Praise for
Losing Your Faith, Finding Your Soul

"David Anderson's profound and personal reflections upon life's perennial pattern of loss and discovery provide insight and encouragement to seekers and believers alike. Wisdom drawn from Anderson's experience and that of many others who have become his companions along the way, make this a rich resource to which the reader will want to return again and again."

—FRANK T. GRISWOLD, former Presiding Bishop,
the Episcopal Church

"In *Losing Your Faith, Finding Your Soul,* David Anderson leads the "spiritually hungry yet suspicious" pilgrim right into the heart of the transformational path. Forcefully, eloquently, and with real pastoral genius, David opens our understanding to a richer life with God beyond conventional faith—a life that, paradoxically, starts at the moment old beliefs fail. He shows that "finding your soul" means awakening to a life of faith that is large enough to embrace the dynamism of human growth in all its pain and ambiguity. This superb and encouraging book meets a huge need. I recommend it wholeheartedly."

—CYNTHIA BOURGEAULT, PhD, Episcopal priest, teacher,
conference leader; author of *The Wisdom of Jesus*

"There's a bracing toughness about this *Pilgrim's Progress* for our time. We live in a culture where the predominant belief is that everything in principle is fixable. (No wonder many of us live lives of puzzling disappointment.) David Anderson confronts us with the great unfixables of love, death, and time. All these themes are forcefully yet gently faced in this remarkable book."

—ALAN JONES, Dean Emeritus of Grace Cathedral, San
Francisco; honorary Canon of the Cathedral of Our Lady
of Chartres; author of *Soul-Making*

"In *Losing Your Faith, Finding Your Soul,* David Anderson says what every thoughtful Christian has realized—faith was meant to be built upon, not enshrined. This book is a tribute to doubters, those seeking honesty, and those in search of a faith forged in failure. There are no flowers here, and no rosy promises, but truth abundant and light for the journey."

—PHILIP GULLEY, author of *Living the Quaker Way*

LOSING YOUR FAITH,

FINDING YOUR SOUL

LOSING YOUR

FAITH,

FINDING YOUR

SOUL

The passage to new life when old beliefs die

David Robert Anderson

CONVERGENT

Losing Your Faith, Finding Your Soul
Published by Convergent Books

Hardcover ISBN: 978-0-307-73120-3
eBook ISBN: 978-0-307-73121-0

Cover design and photo by Mark D. Ford

Published in association with the Sarah Jane Freymann Literary Agency, 59 West 71st St., Suite 9B, New York, NY 10023.

CONVERGENT BOOKS and its open book colophon are trademarks of Random House Inc.

Library of Congress Cataloging-in-Publication Data
Anderson, David, 1956–
    Losing Your Faith, Finding Your Soul : A Guide to Rebirth When Old Beliefs Die / David Robert Anderson.—First Edition.
        pages cm
    ISBN 978-0-307-73120-3—ISBN 978-0-307-73121-0 (electronic)
    1. Faith. 2. Spirituality. 3. God (Christianity) 4. Expectation (Psychology)—Religious aspects—Christianity. I. Title.
    BV4637.A53 2013
    234—dc23

                                                                          2013014289

Printed in the United States of America
2013—First Edition

10 9 8 7 6 5 4 3 2 1

SPECIAL SALES
Most Convergent books are available at special quantity discounts when purchased in bulk by corporations, organizations, and special-interest groups. Custom imprinting or excerpting can also be done to fit special needs. For information, please e-mail SpecialMarkets@ConvergentBooks .com or call 1-800-603-7051

For Pam

O lady, you in whom my hope gains strength…, in all the things that I have seen, I recognize the grace and benefit that I, depending upon your power and goodness, have received.

—Dante Alighieri, *The Divine Comedy,*
Canto XXXI

I often want to say to people, "You have neat, tight expectations of what life ought to give you, but you won't get it. That isn't what life does. Life does not accommodate you, it shatters you. It is meant to, and it couldn't do it better. Every seed destroys its container or else there would be no fruition."

—Florida Scott-Maxwell, *The Measure of My Days*

CONTENTS

THE FIFTH PASSAGE: UNCONDITIONAL SURRENDER

THE SIXTH PASSAGE: HABITS OF THE HEART

Soul Honey

Last night, as I was sleeping,
I dreamt—marvelous error!—
that I had a beehive
here inside my heart.
And that the golden bees
were making white combs
and sweet honey
from my old failures.

—Antonio Machado, translated by Robert Bly

Let me tell you a secret. There is a beehive there in your heart, and the golden bees are dying to make white combs and the sweet honey of ecstasy and fulfillment for you. But those bees need nectar to make their soul honey. They need your old failures, something to work with. They need tears and regret, grief and bitter loss. Anger is great for this honey. So is the special shame and humiliation that comes when our failures go public. Depression, for these golden bees, is the finest nectar.

You don't have to do anything exactly for these white combs to form in your heart. You just have to leave it alone. Remember watching chicks hatch? The teacher had to practically tie your hands behind your back. You wanted to "help" each chick break the shell and emerge into life.

It takes wisdom to understand this paradox: you must be present to your own rebirth and consent to its happening in every moment, but the work of the soul is to stand down in the presence of God, to trust what is happening even though you are worried about the outcome and want nothing more than to jump in and control everything. Just so, the redeeming bees will do their slow and quiet work with your old failures, making in the darkness of their bodies your own sweet salvation. As long as you can leave them alone, trust them, let it happen.

But that is nearly impossible, especially in the early stages of life. Then, unless we have experienced some early loss—an accident that alters our lives, a sickness that robs us of the assumed immortality of youth, or some mistake with awful consequences—we cannot admit to any failures. Frightening emotions like anger and resentment are quickly stuffed in the dark caves tunneling off from the heart. Failures are merely the things we have not yet fixed (and we *will* fix them all). Tears are only for the drying. In our early years it can hardly be otherwise. We are consumed with creating a self, an identity, finding that one magic person, chasing security and success, mastering the world. None of that comes to pass if you just "let it happen." By God, you *make* it happen, and failure is not an option.

For most of us, this is where our early "faith" rests: in the whole system of reward and punishment that promises happiness and blessing to those who work hard, believe the right things, play by the rules, and help others in need. "God" is the one who superintends the whole system and guarantees its just deserts both here and hereafter. Even people who aren't religious buy into this system. Whether they call it fate, karma, kismet, or the laws of the universe, it's the same idea. We spend our early years believing in the system until it fails us, usually somewhere about midlife.

It happens to everyone, though its full realization may not dawn for years. "God" was supposed to remember the sacrifices you made.

He was supposed to save your marriage, protect your job, heal your son. Faced with such disappointment, many retreat into denial because it is too frightening to renegotiate "God." They revise a few key beliefs or assumptions, just enough to keep the old thing going, avoid acknowledging a total loss.

The irony is, those breakdowns and failures are God's repeated attempts to offer us grace and mercy, a new way of being. Mostly, though, we are grace-resistant, too good for mercy. We double down on that old muscular faith and stand our ground.

Yet God is relentless, infiltrating our lives through the very cracks and gashes we are frantic to repair, to plaster over. "The world breaks everyone," Hemingway could see, "and afterwards many are strong at the broken places."[1]

All it takes is one inkling of the divine paradox, that we are saved by our losses, and the whole field reverses. Some strange mystery is at work here, a power you did not invoke and cannot comprehend. Your only job, the most difficult you have ever attempted, is to keep saying yes. The bees of heaven are circling. Let them come.

THE GOOD-BYE GATE

ONE

Ariadne's Thread

After a time, Christian reached the Wicket Gate, and over it was written, "Knock, and it shall be opened unto you."

—John Bunyan, *The Pilgrim's Progress*

In the winter of my fortieth year I was sitting in a doctor's office, squirming to get back to work. I was a very busy pastor, only there to get some meds for my strep throat and get back in the game.

A wise, old nurse popped a thermometer in my mouth. "Let me get your blood pressure," she muttered. I took off my coat and rolled up my left sleeve. The cuff wheezed and crimped my bicep as I stared at the white wall. "What's your usual blood pressure?" the nurse asked me. I didn't know. I'd had my blood pressure taken for years; no one had ever given me a reading. "Well, it's high," she said. "150 over 102." The numbers might as well have been a blowout NBA game. They meant nothing to me, but I could tell immediately that something was wrong.

"I want you to see the doctor, Reverend."

My doctor was kind and upbeat, but after taking my pressure for himself, he had to deliver the news. This was nothing to flirt with. Hypertension was like plugging a 110-watt body into a 220 socket. "Leading cause of stroke." He used words like "heart failure," "aneurysm," and "renal failure." And my numbers were way over the top.

I went home with a prescription for Prinivil. The little blue pill brought my blood pressure down from the danger zone, but it was not the medicine for what really ailed me. What I most needed was to relax, stop working sixteen-hour days, pull back a bit on the throttle. But no doctor could script that, only I could. And I was not ready. Things were going too well. The small church I had begun to lead four years before was now a rapidly growing congregation. Attendance was up. Giving was up. It was growing faster than I could manage, and we had called the first assistant clergy in the church's 120-year history.

Every Sunday the ushers were setting up folding chairs in the aisles, and we knew we had to do something. We were planning a capital campaign to build a new church more than double the size, enlarge the parish hall, add Sunday school classrooms, and build a parking lot. A minister's dreams are made of this stuff. I was a "success." Over the next two years we completed the building plans and raised close to two million dollars. That spring we were lining up building permits and preparing to break ground in the fall. But it all went up in smoke.

At 10:00 p.m. on a Mother's Day night the phone beside my bed rang. There was a fire at the church. I jumped into my jeans and then into the car. When I crested the hill on Route 263, still a mile from the church, the sky was all orange. I groaned as if someone had punched me in the belly.

That night, along with scores of parishioners who had heard the news, I stood on the porch of the house next door and watched it all burn down. The school, the parish hall with its leaded windows and wood-beamed ceilings, and finally the church, built of Pennsylvania fieldstone in 1876. It was all gone now—my life's work. But it got worse. Two days later, federal ATF officials informed me that the fire had been deliberately set. This wasn't just a terrible tragedy; it was a horrible, senseless crime. I fancied myself the victor, but I did not know how to be the victim. I was forty-two years old, approaching the pinnacle of my career, and someone with a gas can and a match had destroyed everything.

This was not what I deserved, not what I was promised. I was emotionally exhausted and spiritually pissed. In public, of course, I was strong and dependable. I preached about forgiving the arsonist. I told people God would only use this to make us better, stronger, more compassionate. But in my lonely moments I was foul, angry. The whole thing was a stupid outrage. A few months later my mother died, and that loss pushed me over the edge. I slid into depression.

The fire that night had been more than a church fire—it was a funeral pyre. What had gone up in tall columns of smoke were my sense of who I was, the sure promise of life, my reliable faith, my comforting hope—all of it gone. Well, most of it. At the peak of my life, when I expected to be strongest in faith, I was weakest. I was losing it. I thought I was finished.

I didn't know it then, but what I thought was an end was in fact a beginning, and a promising one. Gradually, I realized that what was happening to me was universal. One way or another everyone comes to this pyre, loses the familiar old, and gropes for a way forward. That strange and remarkable passage is what I want to share in the pages ahead.

⟍⟍

This is a book for people whose faith has failed them. It's for people who used to believe. People who still pretend to believe, who are still teaching their kids to believe, still going to church. Or not. It is for people who have felt spiritually numb for years, their faith snuffed out with the candle of innocence.

This is a book for people who've walked to the front of a church to surrender their lives to God, maybe more than once. People whose prayers used to be answered (at least most of the time). People who have known Jesus in their hearts for years but wonder now whether he was only a figment of their childhood imagination. Their fixed theological views don't seem so fixed anymore.

I write this for men and women who've lived long enough to hit a few brick walls. For some, I've discovered, that collision comes early. Maybe for you it was at university, or the early years of building a career or raising a family. Maybe a person or an event outside your control tipped you into the suffering years too soon—stole away your comfortable certitudes and left you to contemplate cold, hard reality long before your peers.

Or maybe this is you: You've got a job but haven't made it to the top yet, and it's pretty clear you're never going to. You have a house; it used to be your "dream house," but now the dream looks scuffed and slightly dated. You have a husband or a wife and children, but they all pretty much go their separate ways in the morning. Everyone's stressed. Your marriage is on autopilot, and you're too tired to have sex. You've worked hard, been responsible, saved for college. You took the kids to church until they started playing hockey and soccer on Sunday mornings. You believe in something eternal, but it seems a million miles from where you live. Any faith you had seems powerless before the problems you face and the questions that haunt you in the night. You've hit some crisis that calls into question the whole way you've been living your life. You need to slay a big dragon, and you know you're going to need something more than your old go-to faith.

The paradox that crisscrosses adult faith is that all the liabilities of aging now become your chief assets. Only people who have faltered, lost a step, suffered and died a little are ready for the divine life that cannot be earned or grasped but can only be received as a gift. Right now, all you need to be in line for that gift is a willingness, like Noah, to sail away from the old world—recognize you can't hold on to what's passing away—and trust that God is leading you to a place you cannot yet envision. That's why this first passage is the Good-Bye Gate.

But this is not a book to take away your faith. It is a tract that meets you down at the soul's Lost Luggage counter, to show you how a renewed and deeper faith grows precisely through loss and disillusionment.

For twenty years as a pastor I've had a privileged role as a spiritual guide for men and women trying their best to live lives of faith, lives of depth and meaning. I've been there from birth to death and everything in between. There are always seasons of joy and triumph—I love those times, of course, but it's no secret that these are not the spiritual hot spots. I've learned the hard way that moments of confusion and grief are.

When people are slogging through the Slough of Despond or enduring the Dark Night of the Soul, I've been invited to sit with them, listen, offer advice and support. Maybe they sought me out because they sensed that my being a pastor had not shielded me from the changes and chances of life.

I've found myself sitting with women who wanted another baby because they felt their lives had no purpose once their kids were all in school. With men at the peak of their powers who had been cashiered at work, who bounced like a pinball between rage, indignation, and depression. With couples facing a child's autism or a teenager's drug charges.

Their words echoed my own: "This is not what I expected." "This isn't right." "How could this happen to me?"

Like most pastors or therapists, I look back now and wonder what I could possibly have said to these poor people when I was lost in the same maze with no idea, really, how to find the way home.

It's been a few years. I'm in my midfifties now, and while I don't claim to have arrived, I have learned a few things about this trek. Because I now speak and write about faith lost and found, more people ask me for guidance when they feel lost. If there's even a little receptivity, I invite people to lean into the pain. What are the *spiritual* dimensions of this crisis? When you're done fidgeting with the levers of the time machine and it's clear there's no going back, what are you going to do? What if failure, disruption, and endless changes are part of the divine plan? What if the life you're trying desperately to turn around is in fact dragging you assward through the knothole of glory? What if the mess you're trying to clean up is actually God's masterpiece of nonrepresentational art, bricolaged from all the adventures and ordeals of your life? (And yes, that red is blood.)

Over the years I've worked with many people who have lost their old faith—sometimes in heartbreaking ways—and finally found their souls. Almost all of them got pushed into this backhanded blessing. They didn't get there by being especially good or virtuous. They fell. They got fired. They got sick, or someone they love got sick. They drank themselves into some abyss. They lost a lot of money. The sheriff served them with papers.

For others the fall is more like a long slide. The career plateaus, the children fail to turn out well, collagen dissolves, a herniated disk cripples the signature golf swing. The golden boy fades to brass, and the prom queen falls from grace. It's a gradual descent, but the effect is the same. They're lost. Everything they believed in, the landmarks they steered by, are gone. After that they have to find a new way to live, but how do they do that? Nearly everyone is clueless. Actually, it's worse than that.

Let me explain.

For most people, the eclipse of an old life presents only one challenge: how to get it back. If you come to me or to a therapist, you're looking for help in fixing what's broken, solving the problem, and getting life back to normal. That's a legitimate response in our youth. But those of us who've passed the meridian of life need a push. Can you locate your soul at the bottom of this morass? If the old version of you doesn't work anymore, who are you really? If success has failed you, what actually brings happiness and fulfillment? If what you thought was ultimate turns out to be transient, what's truly eternal? If the poles of your world have been reversed, and the way up is the way down, where do you even start?

Instinctively, many people turn to their faith. And what they dredge up is a huge disappointment. It's usually some relic of adolescence or the ascendant years of early adulthood. Some people gave up on religion and faith soon after those early years. Others have been more or less faithful and still end up completely bollixed.

Early-stage faith is always about polishing the apple for God's desk. It's all about achievement—religious or spiritual performance (being good, helping others, qualifying for heaven), but achievement all the same—which is why it fits perfectly with the first half of life but becomes a serious liability in the second. When you need something to access the realm of mystery and inner power, you reach for your faith and come up with a memory box filled with old beliefs, bromides, rules, and rituals. There's nothing exactly wrong with any of it, except that now it seems antique, sentimental, useless.

Plenty of people have sat in my office, or in the coffee shop where I meet most seekers, and opened that old box. Some feel helpless, others embarrassed. This is when I have to deliver the news: as painful as it is to file for spiritual bankruptcy, it's just the ticket. Adult faith begins with a great big ugly death. You move through this first passage, the Good-Bye Gate. Have a good cry and let's move on.

"Wait just a blessed minute!" comes the retort. "Where do I go from here? *How* do I go from here? If spirituality isn't about being good or doing the right things, if it can't protect me from pain and loss, improve my life, and help me solve my problems, what's the point?"

A suspicious look often follows. "Since I was a kid, people like you—pastors, priests, people in collars and robes—have been telling me that religion is all about being a better person, accepting Jesus, believing the Bible. If I believed in God and tried to be the sort of person God wanted me to be, I'd be happy in this life and find heaven in the next." They don't usually finish the thought, but the look says: "So where do you come off telling me it's all bunkum?"

How do you tell people that everything they've ever believed is important, necessary and—now—behind them? I have often wished I could reach for a guidebook, a map of the soul, to give to people sitting there so lost.

Two summers ago my wife, Pam, and I went hiking in Vermont. We bought a book that detailed scores of beautiful trails in the area and then laced up our boots. We started with the easiest paths, but after the first week we were physically ready for steeper, more rugged climbs. What was not quite so ready was our sense of orientation. The more challenging trails were hardly worn, far less traveled, often obscured by undergrowth. Unlike on the comfy paths, we found no friendly printed signs with arrows. All we had were the trail map and infrequent blazes. Many blazes were weathered and disappeared into the mottle of tree bark. You could get lost, and we did.

Once we wandered so far off the trail that we ended up in the backyard of a small cottage on the edge of the woods. A helpful woman showed us how to get back to the trail. We learned on those advanced hikes how to internalize the directions and landmarks from the trail map. We developed an eye for blazes and a sense of the intervals between them—when to expect the next one.

That's what I want to give people who are lost midfaith—a simple map with directions for exactly *this* section of the trail, detailing major landmarks and tricky turns you're certain to miss without help. No one gave me that map. I was a minister, and yet I wasn't prepared when my steadfast faith buckled beneath me. Half the stuff I had been peddling from the pulpit was true in theory, but I didn't really know what it meant.

When Jesus said, "For those who want to save their life will lose it, and those who lose their life for my sake will find it,"[1] I pretended to get it, but I didn't—not really. Other, less circumspect people lost things, not me. Especially not my life. But after the turbulent years of my early forties, I sensed that my life had somehow gone lost (even if I hadn't set out to lose it), and I had to know the secret of those cryptic words.

I picked up a few books on the stages of faith development and was heartened to discover that my predicament was universal. As psychologist James Hillman says, "A symptom suffers most when it doesn't know where it belongs."[2] I wasn't alone. What was happening to me was part of a predictable pattern of human development. Knowing that universal pattern is like having a map of your life—with an X that says, "You are here."

Of all the books I read on the topic, the one that changed my outlook was James Fowler's classic *Stages of Faith: The Psychology of Human Development and the Quest for Meaning.* I was fascinated by the progression of every stage, from infancy to childhood, from adolescence to the many incarnations of adulthood. But what "spoke to my condition," as the Quakers say, was the midlife breakdown that happened like clockwork. In the lifelong progression of faith, this was the big megillah—and I was in it. What I was experiencing was a systemic collapse. If what I was reading was true, however, it wasn't my fault. In good time, it happens to everybody.

Every human being is equipped from birth with an operating system. It's the basic system that tells you who you are, how to behave, what is good and true and beautiful, how to be a success, how to be happy. No one ever says, "Pardon me while I transfer a few files into your operating system." You're not even aware the system exists. It runs in the background and makes everything else possible, but no one mentions it, just as no one says, "Now I am breathing," or "Now my cerebral cortex is engaging." This operating system serves most of us very well in our early, formative years.

The problem is, this software has a fatal virus. It is programmed to guide us to our peak powers and then to crash. At some point in our lives, what has always worked doesn't anymore. It is as if a curtain is pulled back, and what was always just whirring quietly in the background is now revealed. It *is* a system. And it's broken. We call it *Convention*. The beautiful irony is, it cannot be named or even seen until it crashes.

That's where I was at forty. Maybe that's where you are now at twenty-eight or forty or sixty-two. Improbably, this turns out to be the golden moment.

According to Fowler and the many other prophets of human development, recognizing the pervasive power of that conventional system is key to spiritual growth.[3] We have to recognize it, escape it, transcend it. That is the task of maturity. There are stages before and stages after, but this is the big one.

In earlier years, the transitions flow almost naturally. But getting beyond Convention is like escaping the hideous tractor beam in *Star Trek*. For that we need help.

As I came to understand this, whenever I looked at the adults in my congregation—not to mention my friends, my colleagues, the characters in nearly every book and movie—I found myself concluding, "They're all stuck in Convention." I saw a lot of pain and confusion, a lot of resentment and bitterness. Some tried to keep up religious appearances with a disciplined program of denial; others went cool and cynical. Some were still clinging to the beautiful memories of past faith, which can sometimes be relived but with weaker and weaker claims to reality. If I could help people recognize what was happening—translate the psychological and theological into the terms of everyday life—I might be able to help people escape the conventional trap and find the path to redemption and happiness.

Here I offer six passages that lead the way out of the old, dying form of your faith and into what is new, mysterious, and alive. Beginning with the Good-Bye Gate—the moment when conventional faith breaks down—these passages are designed to lead you through what is often a confusing labyrinth.

This ancient myth may help to illumine the path.

When Theseus volunteers to kill the Minotaur, and so spare the poor Athenian children who will otherwise be fed to this awful beast, he has two problems: killing the half-bull half-man (no small task), and finding his way back. The Minotaur crouches at the center of a vast maze on the isle of Crete. Even if Theseus can find his way to the center of the maze and manage to slay the beast, he will not be able to find his way out. It is Ariadne who comes to Theseus's aid. She gives him a ball of thread, which he ties to the entrance door and unwinds as he twists his way to the center. After dispatching the Minotaur, he follows the thread and winds his way out of the labyrinth.

That is what I have set out to do here. The six passages of this book require something like Ariadne's thread. These are the natural pathways of the soul, six passages every man and woman must make on the way to a mature, adult soul. Yet they lead through confusing and difficult terrain, where the road home is counterintuitive: the right way is often the one that appears wrong. You need a lead to follow.

Like the Cretan labyrinth, these six passages are not a linear progression. Different people will make these moves in different orders; nevertheless, each passage is threaded to another. Finding your way through one opening gives you the wisdom to choose well at the next intersection. What you learn in one passage will help you take other important steps along the way.

Negotiating each passage requires a level of honesty, courage, and trust available only to those who have come to the end of themselves—and then found a small opening, a light, and a way forward. That is why this whole endeavor is cloaked in paradox: our losses turn out to be necessary—and as such, gifts. It's not easy to acknowledge defeat, the end of our best-laid plans, but we are never given a new life until we have released the old one. That pattern of losing-to-find, emptying-to-be-filled, dying-to-be-reborn is the promise that sings through every passage, along every mile of this pilgrimage.

I hope you'll think of me as your Ariadne, offering you a skein of thread, a slender guiding strand, a filament of hope that enables you to turn a corner and keep going when everything in your head is crying, "Go back!"

This ball I hold is woven of many strands. Years of my own experience and that of the men and women I've counseled, together with threads of Merton and Jung, Oliver and Eliot and Dillard. Stories of faith, hope, and love that others have told me along the way, tales of losses that became precious, endings that birthed beginnings. I've collected them like bits of string, woven them together and wound them one by one over the years. They are what inspire and delight me, the only things that keep me going.

Here, take this thread. You'll need it for the passage that awaits.

TWO

The End of Magical Faith

All changes, even the most longed for, have their melancholy; for what we leave behind us is a part of ourselves; we must die to one life before we can enter another!

—Anatole France, *The Crime of Sylvestre Bonnard*

Life is under no obligation to give us what we expect.

—Margaret Mitchell, *Gone with the Wind*

This first passage is as simple as saying good-bye, and just as difficult. I don't know anyone—myself included—who does this well. When people move and leave their home community, they often protest, "I'm not good at saying good-bye." Or they say, "It's only three hours down the road. I'll be back"—when you both know they won't, and even if they do, it will be as visitors. A few honest souls have told me, "I don't *say* good-bye."

But maturing as a man or woman is a movement out of cherished illusions and into plain reality. The greatness of spiritual giants is not that they see visions of the seventh heaven, but that they see what is under their noses. It is that simple.

That's why the first passage out of early-stage faith is a conscious recognition of its loss. You walk through the Good-Bye Gate. You say,

"The faith I inherited as a child is over. I do not know what lies ahead. I know only what is gone." You begin to walk down a very narrow road, in the blessed company of people like Abraham, who left everything and set out for a place to be named later.

The gate is open. Let's go on through.

In 1997 a teenage boy named Frank was horsing around with a bunch of boys who, on a whim, decided to swim the Delaware River. It didn't seem far from the Pennsylvania shore to the Jersey side. And of course it isn't. The problem always is the swift, unseen currents. Frank never made it.

The boy who drowned was a friend of my daughter Maggy, and she was not ready for death. At fourteen she was still a girl and yet… not. She and her close group of girlfriends vowed to keep Frank's memory alive, by taping his picture to their bedroom walls, by listening to his favorite songs, by wearing black day after day.

I knew my daughter was in mourning, but I did not know until months later how deeply that death had shaken her world. One day she said to me, "Dad, I don't believe Frank is really up in heaven somewhere." The boy did not come from a religious home and had no apparent faith. She added, "And I don't think he's in hell either." (At a slumber party the past summer, she had stayed up all night discussing religion with friends, some of whom believed that those who were not "saved" were marked for hell.) After a long silence I said, "I think you're right."

That profound moment led us into a discussion that continued, off and on, for weeks. What she meant by declaring her belief that Frank was neither up in heaven somewhere nor down in hell was that she was no longer a child. Children believed in a magical place quite

literally above the clouds and a hideous place somewhere far underground. Children believed that good people went up and bad people
went down. And she was not a child anymore. One real experience of
grief had, like a private tsunami, swept that world clean away.

What drowned with Frank was Maggy's childhood. That was
what she mourned. The loss hurt, but there was also a hard-won con-
solation. I could see it in her pensive eyes and the defiant pursing of
her lips: she was no longer a little girl. This, apparently, was what it felt
like to approach adulthood. It hurt, but she'd made it this far and she
wasn't going back.

"Now you're ready," I said, "to know a little deeper." And I took
her beyond the literal, into the mystery whispered in metaphor, into
the truth so far beyond it can only be hinted at. The pensiveness still
darkened her eyes, but the defiance had left her lips. I had taken her
into the adult counsels.

This is the first faith you lose: the spiritual form of innocence. Reality
mugs the clean and tidy story of childhood. The magical vision breaks
down, as it did for Maggy. Good people die, and young. Like Holden
Caulfield, you find there is no "catcher in the rye," no invisible angel
to catch the innocents who fall from the cliff. Good and evil used to
be black and white. Just do your very best and you'll be okay; you'll
be rewarded in the end. Now the way of the world seems darker,
inscrutable.

It's usually some heartbreak that drags you mercilessly from innocence to experience. For most of you, it spells the end of juvenile
religious faith, but it doesn't end your spiritual questing. You simply
come to a deeper understanding of life. Your mind, your body is
developing so fast in these years, giving you knowledge, insight, and

experience you simply didn't possess just a few years earlier. Your mind can handle things like symbol and metaphor. Your hormonally charged body surges with passion and what feels for all the world like deep, true love. As an adult-in-training you're ready to graduate to the next level of spiritual awareness. You can begin to sense the depth of human experience—that your deepest joys arise somehow from the place of suffering and loss. You can't fall in love, for example, without *falling*. You can't know heaven without a darker knowledge we call hell.

In these times of crisis, young people like Maggy have a momentary, real vision of the world, but it doesn't last. They don't usually see the universal implications of this one death. They aren't ready for Isaiah's vision, "All flesh is grass."[1] They can't see with Qoheleth, "Vanity of vanities, all is vanity."[2] They just know that the garden wall has been breached. There's rumor of a serpent on the loose. But it's no use thinking about that now; there's an awesome rock concert in the park tonight.

This first transformation, then, is a big one. Almost everyone makes this first jump (a few hang back and insist on living in a spiritual childhood their whole lives), but it isn't the last. Once you leave the wizardly world of childish faith, you get on the road to adulthood. As your body morphs, so does your soul. You ask the big questions: *Who am I? What am I going to be? Why is my family so lame? How fast can I get out of here?*

It's a very me-centered process, and that's just as it should be. The task of life for adolescents and young adults is to separate from home and family, establish an independent identity. Get a job. Get an apartment. Maybe spend some years teaching ESL in Thailand, but eventually settle down. Find love with a soul mate. Get a house. Have a child. Get a real job, something that pays bills and matches contributions to a 401(k). Before you know it, you're mingling awkwardly at your college reunion, wondering where fifteen years went and what happened to everybody's hair.

We all get on that road to adulthood because there's a great big sign at the entrance ramp. It reads:

THIS WAY TO THE GOOD LIFE
Hard Work Ahead
Commitment Required
Big Rewards to Come

The explicit promise of this road is happiness. Ultimate fulfillment. Satisfaction. Peace. And whether you recognize it or not, this is a spiritual quest. You may wander from church and religion in the Beer Pong days of early adulthood, but if, like Paul Tillich, you understand faith as that of "ultimate concern," it never goes away.[3] When you hold a fishing line and the world is utterly still, when death claims someone you love, when a nurse lays a newborn baby in your arms, it's there.

The highway to happiness: that's what you're on in your twenties and thirties. It's a spiritual quest fueled by hard work, faithfulness, and morality. Believe the right things, do the right thing, try to be a good person. That's the way to ensure success. It's called conventional faith, and it works, for the most part. If you doubt that, just check out your friends who stayed too long in Key West, never actually settled down, never got real jobs, never made commitments to anything or anyone beyond themselves. It's not a pretty scene.

The only problem is, it works until it doesn't. Everything's fine until things start to break down, fall apart. You put in long hours, and somebody else gets the promotion. You train for marathons, yet your blood pressure still climbs out of control. Your husband sleeps in another room. Your high school senior is hospitalized for depression.

Now working hard doesn't pay. Being good doesn't protect you. Having faith doesn't make everything all right.

This is how you lose your faith the second time. The promise fails you—it was all a lie.

I suppose some people waltz through life without suffering, then read *The God Delusion* and suddenly lose their faith. But that's not what I see day after day in my work. It's always some loss, some undeserved suffering; it's the outrageous—sometimes cruel—disparity between our vision of a secure, God-governed world and the way life actually turns out.

It's the oldest question known to man. *Why?*

Peter De Vries, the writer and novelist, grew up in a good midwestern Dutch Reformed household. He went to church. Went to Calvin College in Grand Rapids. Eventually he joined the staff of the *New Yorker,* where he worked for over forty years. De Vries dedicated his 1959 novel, *Through the Fields of Clover,* "To Emily with Love." Emily was his daughter, suffering with leukemia, who eventually died at the age of ten. De Vries wrote to J. D. Salinger, "One trip through a children's ward, and if your faith isn't shaken, you're not the type who deserves any faith."[4] That's a voice from way beyond conventional belief. It's a man whose faith has been shaken, and he's no longer trying to whistle his way past the children's ward. De Vries is right. You don't deserve faith (adult faith, that is), if the old credulity hasn't been shaken.

Usually, it's suffering that does the shaking.

The couple sat in my office. It had taken everything I could muster to get them both there, sitting together. It was a second marriage for both, and after the birth of their own daughter and eight good years, he had lost his job. Six months later, the severance ran out. All the little problems snowballed. Now the bitterness and mistrust went so deep neither could look at the other. It took an hour to get them to agree to one therapy session.

"You need serious counseling," I said, "but that's not the end of it. This isn't just a problem to be solved. It's a spiritual crisis, and if you're awake—if you can stay with the pain and not bail on it—this can actually push you to a deeper level."

The husband just shook his head. "I'm losing my marriage, and I'm losing my faith. My grandfather always said, 'All things work to-gether for good, to those who love God,' and that was always my theme song when things got tough. Now when I call my dad and talk about the job search, he says, 'Remember what your grandfather said… All things work together for good. God has a plan.' But I don't think I believe it anymore."

In a moment like that, all you can do is listen. Take off your shoes. This is holy ground. A man or woman has come to the end of that great highway to happiness, and there's nothing there. Every-thing that person has believed in is lost. It's an awful moment, but it's pulsing with divine energy.

We pass through the Good-Bye Gate when we muster enough courage to step into and then through our souls' losses. Strangely, this farewell gate opens into a place of new awareness. When most people arrive here, however, they assume it's the terminus—game over. They walk away. But if you can somehow walk into the loss, you're in line for an adult soul. R-rated faith begins only when the G-rated stuff ends, only when the God of our childhood dies. For Jews, Christians, Muslims, Hindus, Buddhists, the essential paradox of faith is: *you can't find it until you lose it.* "Losing your faith" is the gate to adult spirituality. But so many people get to the Good-Bye Gate…and stop.

Whether we call it salvation, moksha, enlightenment, nirvana—all the great religions teach us to step *through* that gate. True, most faith communities don't use that language much, but the secret is al-ways there for anyone ready to hear it. When you reach the end of what you used to know as faith, the path you were on suddenly peters out. You need a new, deeper truth.

I always envision this the way Dante described his own midlife crisis in the *Divine Comedy* (and for a medieval guy, age thirty-five was getting up there).

> In the middle of the journey of our life
> I came to myself within a dark wood
> Where the straight path was lost.[5]

Everybody comes to the end of his first, enchanted faith, though I have to say that not everyone—in Dante's terms—comes to himself in that dark forest. But if you do, you will invariably come to that gate, which is really just the edge of that forest darkness. Standing there, you can go in two directions: either into the darkness or out of it. Life—your life— depends on this decision.

The simplest, most sensible decision is to flee the darkness. You stand there in the last sliver of fading light and think, *What a long and sad journey this has been. I believed in some invisible world and a God who watched over me. How embarrassing! I went along with all this rigmarole, and it turns out to be a hoax. I thought if I lived my life right, if I was faithful, prayed just a little, and tried to help others, I'd find some meaning in life—I'd find peace and fulfillment. Instead, I feel like I've been lied to.* That's where faith ends. You chuck it. You're not going to get snookered again. You'll believe only what makes sense, only what you can prove.

The other direction is in—into the dark umbra. It makes no sense to step into a dark unknown, but once you realize you've spent your whole life doing the sensible, socially approved thing and it's landed you at the end with nothing, you may just be ready to do the "senseless" thing.

You stand there in the shadow and something pulls you in. You don't actually do this yourself; you allow it to happen *to you*. Instead of running from failure and loss, you lean into it. Then it's as if you drop through the bottom of it.

This may sound rarefied, but it's simply what happens in a thousand church halls and basements every week when people in Twelve Step programs get down to business. These are folks who've run from the darkness their whole lives, until one day they do a hara-kiri and fall into the whole mess. Amazingly, they keep telling me, they drop through the bottom and into a wondrous new world.

After going through a horrific ordeal with spinal cancer, the novelist Reynolds Price wrote his autobiography, *A Whole New Life*. Ten years after his cancer diagnosis—years of struggling to get his old life back—he says it would have been a great favor to him if someone had walked up to his hospital bed right at the start and said, "Reynolds Price is dead. Who will you be now?"[6]

Pronouncing yourself dead happens to be the prerequisite of all faith traditions (St. Paul says flatly, "I die daily," and Zen master Maezumi Roshi suggests, "Why don't you die now and enjoy the rest of your life?"[7]), but it makes absolutely no sense. So I say it again: if you're not ready to take this step, it will just seem loony. Because it *is*. Who would believe it's the passage to life?

You may be feeling like you've been invited to a pretty flaky party, wondering how you could get your coat and leave without being noticed. All this good-bye business. The end of faith, the end of God, pronouncing yourself dead. That's a little extreme, a little weird, frankly.

Maybe give it one more chapter.

THREE

Cold-Eyed Riley

How did it get so late so soon?
It's night before it's afternoon.
December is here before it is June.
My goodness how the time has flewn.
How did it get so late so soon?

—Dr. Seuss

It was a cool spring Saturday morning in April, and I was leading a retreat at a monastery. There was a knock at my door; I opened it, and there stood Riley. He wanted to speak with me. I invited him to come in. A tall man in his midfifties, he was slightly agitated as he took his seat, wringing his hands, then covering his mouth as he gazed at the floor. I gave him a moment to gather himself.

Something had happened. He did not know how to speak of it. He had told no one. "Why don't you begin at what feels like the beginning," I said.

"It began last night," Riley told me.

Our retreat group had come in the previous afternoon, registered at the front desk, received our room assignments, and settled in. It was an annual retreat, and every year we had a little soiree on Saturday night after dinner. People brought bottles of wine and soft drinks as well as cheeses, fruit, and snacks. The monk in charge of guests invited us—as always—to put our Saturday stash in the big cooler down in the basement. Most of us put our bags in our rooms and put our drinks and food in the cooler as soon as we checked in. Riley had not done this. After we had all said good night and gone to our rooms, Riley was unpacking his bags and found his six-pack of St. Pauli Girl N.A. ("It's not that I'm in the Program; alcohol just does funny stuff to my brain.")

He left his room to find the refrigerator, asking directions of a monk in the hallway. He was to walk all the way to the other end of the building and go into a closet on the right where he would find a stairwell. "Why you had to go into this closet to find the stairwell seemed odd…" But this was an old Gothic monastery, built more than a century ago. I had been down that dark stairwell the day before, stashing my (non-N.A.) wine in the basement cooler. I knew exactly what he was describing.

Riley descended the stairwell and found a stainless steel door. *This must be the walk-in cooler.* He opened the door. There was a light switch on the outside. He turned it on. Looked inside. Where to put his six-pack? There was no room on the shelves. At the far end (this thing was about six feet wide and twelve feet long), he noticed some open space. So he walked to the end, placed his six-pack on a low shelf, and turned to walk out. He took one step and saw the door slowly swinging toward him until it latched.

A frisson of fear rippled through him. Riley walked to the door and saw an inside handle. Thank God. He gripped it, but he couldn't see how it worked. Did you pull it up or push it down? He pulled, he pushed. Nothing. He rattled the handle as hard as he could. Nothing. The thing was jammed.

He paused and looked around. "That's when I noticed the things on the shelves were frozen. This was not a cooler. It was a freezer.

"My first thought was, *It's okay. All you have to do is yell, and someone will hear.*" He yelled and screamed, encased in a foot of freezer insulation. In a moment of terror he realized how bad this was. He was underground, on the far end of the monastery. It was night. Most people were in their rooms—all the way at the other end. They would never hear him.

Riley heaved on the latch handle. Still stuck. He started to pound on the door. "It was stainless steel, with a diamond pattern—the kind you see on truck bed liners. This freezer had been built like a prison." He pounded. He kicked. Riley is six feet seven inches tall; he's a big man. "I pounded furiously, like I was possessed."

Here he raised his hands. I saw the raw wounds and dried blood on the fleshy bottoms of his fists.

Then it happened. The light activated by the outside switch was right above the door. "All my pounding must have finally broken the filament." Riley stood in total blackness.

"Were you cold?" I asked in a half-whisper.

He had slipped out of his room last night in pants and a T-shirt and shoes without socks. "But I wasn't thinking about the cold. I was standing there in the dark, listening to the sound of my labored breath and thinking, *I'm going to die in this freezer.* And it was such a stupid way to die—such a dumb, idiot way to die! I thought about my wife. I thought about my children, hearing the news."

The sudden darkness nearly broke Riley's spirit. In total blackness there was no way to devise an exit. All sense of space collapsed. Riley was totally alone, cut off even from himself. In panic he began to pound again.

I asked how long. "It seemed like hours, but it was probably more like twenty or twenty-five minutes. I kept pounding and pounding, kicking, throwing my body against the door." In exhaustion he stopped, panting in the dark. He felt like crying and vomiting at the same time.

"In the darkness I prayed. Five words. *Oh God, please help me.* After I finished my prayer, I opened my eyes. There at the top of the door was a thin crack of light; then a line of light slid down the side of the door, and it slowly swung open. I watched dumbfounded. I stepped out into the hallway. I just assumed someone had finally heard me, so as I stepped out, I was talking to the person on the other side of the door. But when I looked, there was no one there. I was terrified: *no one there!*"

Riley went to his room and lay on his bed.

"Did you call your wife?" I asked.

"No. I was ashamed. Confused. I'm not sure myself what happened to me. I'm not exactly a cynic, but I'm pretty skeptical. I'm a computer scientist, for God's sake—I don't know how to account for this. I don't know what it means—what I'm supposed to *do.*"

We sat for a long time. A vernal breeze fluttered the drapes at the window. Birdsong floated in the air. Riley was alive, and he didn't know how. Or why.

———

After Riley left my room, I sat for a long time alone. The waves of his story rolled over me. It was the classic midlife horror movie. All of us with a touch of gray feel trapped. We're stuck in our prison cells. We're not sure how we ended up here, but we can't escape. It's like throwing your body at a steel door. In your twenties you could've blown this sucker off its hinges, no problem. But now both your knees have been scoped, and you've got a herniated disk and a bad rotator cuff. All your struggle only bloodies the door.

Then there was the absurdity. Another big midlife theme. *After all I've done to make something of myself, I could die like a fly trapped between a screen and a window.* The struggle is not noble or heroic. There are no rules. You can do everything right, try to find God (even go on retreat to a monastery!), and the scullery kid will still find your frozen corpse when he goes to defrost the breakfast bagels. Riley did not emerge triumphant like Rambo or clever-cool like MacGyver. He stood there shaking like a wounded, confused animal.

That image clutched my mind. For those of us who've lived a few years, it's like ghost stories around the campfire. *Hear about the guy riding his bike in a triathlon? Swerved to avoid a turtle in the road, fell, hit his head, and died. Instantly.* All the salt-and-pepper heads lean in a little closer. *My sister told me about this woman she works with, just made a partner in the firm. She went in for a routine appendectomy, got some weird infection that no antibiotic can touch, and now she can't even feed herself.* All the crow's-footed eyes bug out. It's not just confronting your mortality...no, it's pondering the randomness of it all.

All of this was crashing around Riley like incoming mortar shells. He was in shock. But what impressed me was his capacity for focus. He could stay with the feelings of anxiety and confusion. He didn't stuff the whole experience and try to move on. He sensed the *spiritual* dimension of the moment—that is, his whole ordeal was a death and resurrection. He was on the outside of his life looking in. It's not every day you find yourself clawing at the lid of your own coffin, and since only a fool lets a crisis go to waste, Riley was now hypersensitive. What was the meaning of it all, and what was he supposed to do about it?

This is what faith is supposed to be about: life and death. It's supposed to help you understand, however dimly, what things *mean,* and then what you are to *do*—how you are to live. But when we reach the messy middle of life, or grow older than our youthful years in the midst of change and loss, the old belief systems break down. We're up against the big issues now: *Who am I? How the hell did I get here? How do I get out?* When we need it, religion doesn't help. All the truisms of Sunday school seem stupid at a naked moment like this. All the assurances of heaven leave us abandoned on earth. The Golden Rule is fine when your biggest problem is a selfish friend, but when it feels like you and your little boat are headed over the waterfall, you need to get real—fast. *Help!*

Riley impressed me because he was ready. "When the student is ready, the teacher appears." Not until. It may be too much to say that religion—faith, spirituality—is wasted on the young, but not by much. The simple, single message of all the great spiritual traditions is this: God's new life is waiting to be born in you, but it waits upon your death. Not just the demise of your body (we'll get to the so-called afterlife later), but the death of your *self,* the person you've worked so hard to become. *That's* what has to go. And the beauty is, life has a way of bringing us there whether we like it or not. We have to live long enough, however, for things to start falling apart, for dreams and illusions to burn off, for reality to set in. Some young people, facing significant reversals, have developed old souls, but the callow are not yet ready to let it go.

I used to read the Bible and wonder how Jesus could so easily detach from the rich young man who comes to him with this deep, earnest request:

"Good Teacher, what must I do to inherit eternal life?"[1]

He's not asking about life after death. A better translation of "eternal life" would be something like "the life of the ages." He's asking the perfect question. *How do I find divine life, ultimate truth, perfect fulfillment?*

"You know the commandments," Jesus replies, "you know the rules as well as I do. Have you kept the rules?"

"Yes, I've done all that, and there's still something missing. There must be some secret, and I think you know it."

"Well," says the Master, "there *is* one more thing. Go sell everything you own, take the money, give it to the poor, and then come follow me. *That's* living."[2]

The man walks away—and Jesus lets him go! If someone came to me with a question like that, I'd keep at it. I'd chase him down. Maybe there's another way to explain this to you. You don't literally have to sell everything—it's a metaphor, you know? You just have to come to a place where all that stuff doesn't matter to you anymore. See?

But Jesus lets him walk. And I get it now. The man's not ready. The standard commentary on this story always focuses on the man's wealth. Maybe it's because he's rich—we're all seduced by materialism—but I think it's because he's young. It's not his fault, really. He just doesn't get it.

In his memoir, *Report to Greco,* Nikos Kazantzakis recalls his early years. Even then, the Greek philosopher, novelist, poet was a God-haunted man. He is searching, unsure of his vocation, needing some message from God. One summer the young Kazantzakis climbs Mount Athos to visit a monastery. There he encounters an old monk, Father Makários who has a reputation for deep wisdom. In one remarkable exchange, the young Kazantzakis asks the monk, "Do you still wrestle with the devil?"

"Not any longer, my child," Father Makários replies. "I have grown old, and he has grown old with me. He doesn't have the strength...."

The young man assumes that the battle must be over, that he now lives in ease.

Not so, replies Father Makários. Now, he explains, "I wrestle with God."

"With God!" exclaims the young man. "And you hope to win?"

"I hope to lose, my child."[3]

That exchange between anxious youth and wise experience depicts the radical difference between the two halves of life. In the first half we do battle, as it were, with the devil. We see life as a struggle, trying to make sense of all our aspirations and urges, trying to get it all, savor it all, save it all. It's a struggle, and we mean to win. But in the second half of life, the struggle reverses dramatically. Now, like

Jacob at the Jabbok, we wrestle with God and hope to lose. The task is wholly paradoxical, and the young who have not been through the fire have no idea how to engage this. What they don't know is that the only way you get here— like Jacob, broken by his own stratagems—is by some failure or loss so big it brings down your whole system with it. What they can't know is how beautifully blessed it feels when you've been bested by God, finally to surrender.

When Riley first sat with me and told his story, he had hardly the soul of Father Makários. He was still shaking. He didn't know what his ordeal meant, but he knew it was not just a scare to be gotten over. It was a like a dream so full of archetypes and obvious symbols that its message could not be avoided. You may not know *what* it means, but you know *that* it means! Riley was clearly a man with a second-half-of-life soul.

The old Baptist prophet Carlyle Marney once spoke to a religious group at Duke University in the 1960s. When a student asked Dr. Marney to speak about the resurrection of the dead he replied, "I will not discuss that with people like you."

"Why not?" said the student.

"I don't discuss such matters with anyone under thirty," Marney said. "Look at you, in the prime of life—never had you known honest-to-God failure, heartburn, solid defeat, brick walls, mortality. So what can you know of a dark world which only makes sense if Christ is raised?"[4]

Carlyle Marney would definitely have discussed that life-or-death question with my friend Riley. Jesus would have been eyeball to eyeball with him. He knew honest-to-goodness failure, heartburn, solid defeat, brick walls, mortality. He was ready.

If you know that dark world, and sense that what you once thought spelled the end was somehow writing a prologue, you are passing through that Good-Bye Gate. You are ready too.

FOUR

The System

The machine has got to be accepted, but it is probably better to accept it rather as one accepts a drug—that is, grudgingly and suspiciously. Like a drug, the machine is useful, dangerous and habit-forming. The oftener one surrenders to it the tighter its grip becomes.

—George Orwell, *The Road to Wigan Pier*

Don't let the world around you squeeze you into its own mould.

—Romans 12:2 (Phillips)

If you hope to make this passage out of an old and dying faith and into something alive, you must know what you are up against. The reason you and I remain trapped in that old version of faith, long after it makes sense to be done with it, is because there are blind, powerful forces that wish to keep us there.

Like me, you probably steer clear of conspiracy theories. Nevertheless, I am bound at this point to tell you of a vast conspiracy against every human being, including you. Stay with me on this one, please.

It's like *The Matrix*. That movie series still captures people by the millions (including me) because it hints at something we all suspect. The world is being run by machines we created, and the so-called life we're all consumed with is actually a weird simulacrum, a cleverly engineered dream sequence that everybody assumes is real. But it's not. The heroes and heroines are those who refuse to live an ersatz existence. They're unafraid to take on the system, the machine, the Matrix—and fight for their true lives.

Something very like that is true in the spiritual realm, and you can't make any progress on this human odyssey unless you get this. At the very outset of *The Matrix,* Neo is given a choice. He is offered two pills. Take the little blue pill, and you'll slip happily back into the dream life with no memory of having suspected anything. You're safe. Take the red pill, and the journey continues, the search for truth is engaged, but no one can guarantee the outcome. No security here.

This is the point where you have to choose your pill. That's if you believe in this vast conspiracy. What am I talking about?

It's the whole conventional system, but it's not some dark cabal. It's run by the nicest, most loving, caring people in the world. They mean well. They've been nurturing you since you were a child. At considerable cost, they protected you, kept you safe. When they saw you confused in adolescence, they're the ones who helped you find something you were good at, gave you an identity and a sense of belonging, showed you how to be a young woman or man. When wild instincts arose and you drifted in with the wrong people, they reined you in. Tough love, they called it. They wanted you to be safe, normal. People who stick out are laughed at. They wanted you to be happy, fit in, get into the best school, meet the right mate, get the killer job, see the Piazza Navona at twilight. All they ever wanted was your success. True, they also wanted you to reflect well on them and on your hometown. But really, they loved you.

Every good parent, teacher, aunt or uncle, mentor, coach, rabbi, priest, or imam does this for children and young people in their care. To fail in this responsibility would be well nigh criminal. My parents did this for me, and even now I am doing the same for my two daughters. It's been like this since the Bronze Age. And because it's a path universally followed, it has no name and no one speaks of it. It's not even considered a path—as if there were alternatives. It's just the only road that comes through this town.

What you have to understand, before you take one of those pills, is the tragic beauty of this system. Conventionalism is the perfect gift for children and young people—young adults, even. First of all, when you are childishly ignorant or when you are drunk on your own hormones or somebody's beer, conventionalism saves you from self-destructing. Then later, it helps you rise to great heights of personal mastery, moral goodness, and human achievement. And if, as Franciscan spiritual guide Richard Rohr suggests, you spend the first half of life building your tower, and the second half trying to descend,[1] you can thank your lucky stars for the system that helped you to rise and build that tower. Otherwise you'd have nothing to jump from. And the descent—*that* is the inaugural act of adult spiritual life.

But here's the rub. The community that nurtures you and brings you to the pinnacle of your tower will always try to keep you there. It's that safety thing again (the conventional system is obsessed with security). It will walk you around the penthouse, show you the unparalleled views, pour you a glass of Dom Pérignon, and say, "Congratulations. You've worked hard to achieve this. You can do a lot of good for a lot of people right here. Besides, look at all the loved ones counting on you. Now, be sensible. Who would forsake all this for a death leap into nothingness?" The tragic beauty is, the loving system can't help but hold you; it cannot let you go, cannot allow you to descend. The blessing becomes the curse.

In the opening scene of *The Graduate,* Benjamin Braddock is uneasily greeting guests at his parents' home in a wealthy suburb of Los

Angeles. It's a graduation party, and he is the center of attention. All the men and women roaming this party, highballs in hand, are of his parents' generation. "Good job in college," they say, clapping him on the back. "You'll go far." "You'll be as successful as your old man!"

The graduate is deeply troubled. For the first time he's seeing his family as part of a system. He's suddenly conscious of all the unspoken values and norms, the great expectations to follow the family path. Until now he assumed that he had chosen his own path, his own values, his own lifestyle; now he realizes that the system has chosen him. During adolescence, he was blissfully unaware of other possible worlds. Doesn't everyone live like this? Now he's beginning to recognize his own home, family, and culture objectively. He steps outside the circle and examines his life like a tourist or an anthropologist would. And what he sees both disturbs and empowers him: it no longer defines him.

Benjamin's attempt to step away from that system and into a new identity of his own is the rising action of the movie. You might think that a young man's decision to leave his mainstream, establishment family (after all, Benjamin is not from some Amish or Mennonite subculture) would be met with a shrug from Mom and Dad—"Live and let live!" Hardly. The power of *The Graduate* is its plain depiction of the coercive and, literally, seductive power of the system. The siren call of Mrs. Robinson—the wife of his father's law partner— symbolizes the unconscious power and intent of the whole system. At all costs, it wants to lure back to the fold anyone who begins to challenge its basic premise and to imagine a life beyond it. The further pathos of it all comes as we realize that Mrs. Robinson and most adults in the culture need to capture the young man not for his sake, but for theirs. Since they were not able to step beyond these boundaries and are eternally trapped, this young one must join them in their suffering. His escape threatens to indict the whole system and its long tradition.

When I first met Peter, I knew there was something different about him. He was a business consultant who worked in corporate America, but he had about him a quiet aura of knowledge—as if he knew the secret. Peter was on the leadership board of the first church I pastored. He was a few years older than I was, but he was far wiser. As I spent more time with Peter, I found out what he knew.

"When I was a teenager," he told me, "I didn't want to grow up to be my father. I was a dreamer. I wanted to change the world—to make a difference. And my father would scream at me, 'Grow up and face reality!' By which he meant, 'Stop dreaming about making things different and better; stop imagining that the world might work in a different way.'

"I think he hated being a dentist, but that was the family profession. He was terrified by my questions, my defiance.

"I left home and tried to find a new kind of freedom. I studied psychology and worked in the field of psychodrama. I was good at this, and it wasn't dentistry! I was gaining success consulting with hospitals, universities, and corporations. People in the field knew my name.

"But then my business partner—and best friend—got pancreatic cancer and died. And my wife started to feel unhappy, sort of untethered. Her father killed himself on our wedding anniversary, and she sank into black depression. I was a psychological wizard, but I was powerless to help her. The only person who could have helped me, the only one I could talk to, was my business partner. And he was dead.

"In the middle of all this I was gaining national attention for my work. I was a rising star, yet I was terrified by my success—since I knew how powerless I really was.

"I thought I was living this nonconformist life and that I'd escaped the system my father believed in. But national prominence couldn't save me from personal panic. In many ways, I realized, I had become just like my dad.

"That's when I started drinking hard. I was in a rage that things weren't going the way I needed them to go, and I was helpless. I was a proud, cocky atheist. I had rejected the judgmental Presbyterian church of my childhood, so I had no spiritual anchor.

"I was this amazing change agent at work, but at home I couldn't do a thing to pull my wife out of her depression. So I wound up having an affair. Living a lie, the guilt of it all made me drink even heavier, until finally the woman I was seeing on the side was so appalled by my condition she wouldn't come near me.

"It all came to a head when my father got cancer. My addiction was clear by now to everyone but me, and in his dying days my dad pronounced me a total failure.

"I went home one day, got a shotgun out of the attic, loaded it, and stuck the barrel in my mouth. I had my finger on the trigger. I wanted so badly to die. End this. But then I got this message: *This is not for you to do.* I didn't know who it was, but I knew it had complete authority and I put the gun down."

At that point Peter had one phone call in him. He reached out to a psychiatrist colleague who admitted him to a hospital ICU for alcohol poisoning. He nearly got his wish—he almost died. But in the end, he walked, literally, from the hospital to his first AA meeting.

Peter had rejected one system only to be captured by another. He had "made it," but all the success in his little world could not fill the gaping hole inside him. As he later discovered, that soul longing could only be satisfied by the One who spoke those words, *This is not for you to do.*

Peter chose the red pill. In some sense, of course, he had no choice. The truth was thrust upon him. And he knew it. He was like Benjamin Braddock, like Neo. Through no virtue or effort of his own, he had seen behind the veil. It was a knowledge born of sorrow, but he knew there was no life inside the invisible matrix. It would be harder to live outside the system, but his freedom was more than worth the price.

Peter's life story reminds us that the loss of faith we endure is not merely the evaporation of our dewy-eyed belief; it is also the stunning disclosure of a whole false system in which we were completely invested. And it demonstrates what a gift this loss really is. In the poetry of the ancient Easter liturgy, it was the *felix culpa*—the "fortunate fall."

That's why I stand at this intersection waving a red flag. If you miss this, the only spirituality you can pursue is the sunny, self-help version that promises a little blue pill and the prompt restitution of your old dream life. When you get this, though, you'll know how lucky you are to have fallen, and you'll know that your place in the world will always be a little off the main road, slightly underground.

You'll be something like Christian from John Bunyan's classic *The Pilgrim's Progress*. For days and days his soul is troubled, until finally he realizes that he must set out on his pilgrimage. He lives in a city called Destruction, and until now it hadn't occurred to him that there was anything particularly alarming about that. Everybody else in town seems just happy as clams in Destruction. Even his wife and children think he's been acting a little weird lately. They think he might be off his meds. When Christian finally sees the system for what it is, he flees Destruction crying, "Life! Life! Eternal Life!"[2]

When you see your own city cold like that, you'll be solitary, finding true kinship only in others who feel the same urgency about leaving town.

There's an old Hasidic story about a king who faces a terrible dilemma. All the grain his people have just harvested is found to contain a poison so powerful that anyone who eats it will go utterly mad. Since this is the only food supply for the coming year, the awful prospect the king foresees is an empire in which everyone is insane. He must decide. Should the people not eat the grain and die? Or should they eat it and go mad?

There was still some of the previous year's harvest in the royal granary, so at least the sovereign could eat safely for a year. But the king did not want to be a sane ruler of a mad kingdom. Finally he made his decree. All the people—king included—should eat the poisoned grain. But one man would not. The prophet would eat only from the good grain because, the king reasoned, the whole realm must have *someone* to remind them that they had all become utterly mad.[3]

If you want to find your adult soul, you must become something like that prophet. You have to understand the systemic nature of the mess you're in.

Novelist William Burroughs once wryly remarked, "After one look at this planet, any visitor from outer space would say, 'I WANT TO SEE THE MANAGER.'"[4] The trouble is, you and I are not from outer space. We don't see it. There have always been prophets standing at the edges of society, calling out the truth. We roll our eyes. We don't even hear the prophecy coming from our own mouths. The terms we most often use to describe the lives we lead are *crazy busy, surreal, out of control, unreal,* and *insane.* We're caught in some maelstrom of madness from which there seems no escape.

There *is* an escape. To find it, though, you must seek it. You must be single minded and wholehearted. Like Christian, you must be passionate for "Life! Life! Eternal Life!" It's okay to feel lost, without a clue where to turn. Remember the thread, the slender filament that Theseus trails along behind him as he creeps deeper and deeper into the labyrinth, the thread he follows as he winds his way out. That line you hold in your hand is simply knowledge—an awareness of what you must do. *The way in is the way out.* You must descend into the labyrinth and come face to face with the beast at the center. Many people are afraid to do this. They don't want to know about the system—better to remain blissfully ignorant. But you must take that next step. And you can, because you know that once you've reached the center, there is a path to freedom. It is a gracious ascent, reserved for those who will make the descent.

The whole intent of the first passage—the Good-Bye Gate—is to leave the old, conventional world behind. If you are going to escape the grip of the matrix, you need an inner personal strength that will enable you to break away. You need a powerful new self. That is the focus of the second passage—Stand Apart—and the very next chapter.

But it will make no sense unless you take this red pill. Now.

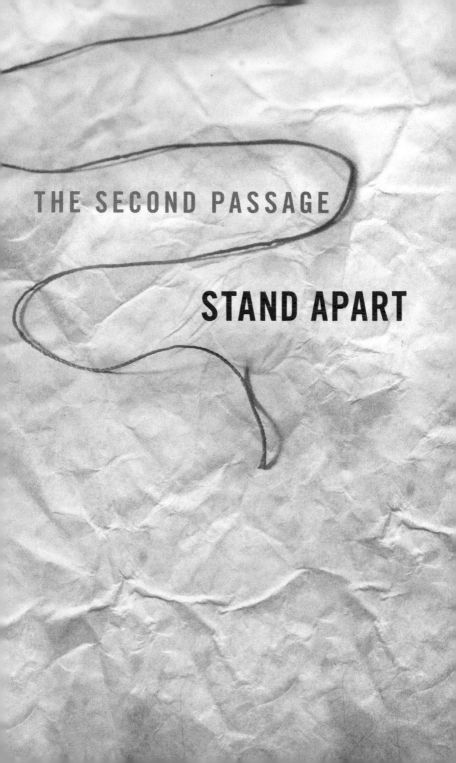

THE SECOND PASSAGE

STAND APART

FIVE

Now I Become Myself

Wizard: Oh! Pay no attention to that man behind
the curtain. The Great and Powerful—
Oz—has spoken—

Dorothy: Who are you?

Wizard: Well, I—I—I am the Great and Powerful—
Wizard of Oz.

Dorothy: You are?

Wizard: Uh—yes.

Dorothy: I don't believe you!

Wizard: No, I'm afraid it's true. There's no other
Wizard except me.

Scarecrow: You Humbug!

Lion: Yeah!

Wizard: Ye-s-s-s—that's exactly so—I'm a humbug.

Dorothy: Oh—you're a very bad man!

Wizard: Oh, no, my dear. I'm—I'm a very good man.
I'm just a very bad Wizard.

—Noel Langley, Florence Ryerson, and Edgar Allen
Woolf, *The Wizard of Oz;* based on the book by
L. Frank Baum

t's a summer family tradition to spend a day at Hersheypark. When
the kids were younger, we spent a lot of time on the Tilt-A-Whirl
and the carousel horses, but we always stood in line for the sea lion

show. So now, years later when we spend most of our time on rides with names like Tower of Terror with a ten-plus g-force, we still go for the sea lions. They're darling, talented, and capable of unbelievable stunts.

I guess I always knew about the little fish treat, but this past summer it was all I could see. Pipin and Nemo were balancing on one front flipper, flying through hoops, dancing with the trainer, and we were all applauding—the little kids squealing with delight. That's when the trainer, who wore a little treat bag on her belt, slipped Pipin and Nemo a fish. Each time they successfully performed a trick, they'd get an immediate reward.

These creatures weren't really dancing, of course. They were performing a series of movements that they knew would produce a fish. It's such a good show—one we stand in line to see—because the sea lions look like they're having such fun. These talented performers who love to be in front of an audience seem almost human. But this summer all I could see was the little fish treat. Pipin and Nemo were just deep-sea circus monkeys. Anything for a herring.

Somewhere in our faith journey, we all have a sea lion moment. You see how you've spent years jumping through hoops, balancing a ball on your nose, not because it's really who you are, but because you've always done it and the system rewarded you for your performance. But when you've done that for ten or twenty years, you start to ask yourself, *Whose approval am I working for? What do I really believe?* Suddenly you see it: you've spent most all your life taking direction from other people. *They* have told you what to believe in, what to work for, what to value, how to live your life. You don't want to end your life like Sinclair Lewis's George Babbitt, the middle-aged real-estate broker who has everything. He lives, after all, in the midwestern town of Zenith. He's reached the top. But on the last page of *Babbitt,* George is speaking to his son Ted, who cannot follow in his father's steps. He wants to leave college and head off on his own way. "Dad, I can't stand it anymore," the boy says. "Maybe it's all right for some fellows. Maybe I'll want to go back some day, but me, I want to get into mechanics." Babbitt, seeming old and subdued, says, "I've never done a single thing I've wanted to in my whole life!"[1]

The Good-Bye Gate brings us naturally to a second passage, leading from dependency to self-possession. As you start separating from the whole worn-out system, you discover that where there is supposed to be a self, there really isn't.

Politicians often attempt to define their opponents before they can define themselves. In a subtle way, that's what your family did for you when you were young. And they weren't the only ones. Your job defined you. Then it was being a mother or a father. Before long it was the neighborhood you lived in, the church you attended, and the political party you inherited. You wonder, *How did this happen?* It's like standing in front of a mirror dressed in what feels like an odd costume and thinking, *Who picked these out for me?* The first movement away from convention leads inevitably to this second passage: Stand Apart. It's the moment when you step out, plant your flag.

This is very different from the adolescent version of "Nobody tells me what to do!" That is merely a nervous act of rebellion, a need to be anything but "them." Young people find external markers—clothes or hairstyles, music or friends—that mark them as different. But it's not an authentic, inner transformation. By contrast, this new identity is not something you create externally; rather, it's something you simply uncover. It's you. But after years of going along with the program, that self is almost totally buried. Finding that first edition of yourself takes a long time (more about that in the next passage: Deep Dive), but it has to start somewhere, and this is it. You begin by taking charge of your own life. Stand apart.

My first sea lion moment came in my thirties. I was raised in a conservative farming town in South Dakota. The fifth of seven children. We worked hard and didn't complain. My father sold and repaired televisions, and I reported to the shop on Saturdays to sweep the floors and pull weeds from the parking lot. Farmers would come in on Friday nights to do their shopping and pick up the tractor radios they had left with my father for repair.

We believed in education and music. After school my mother made me do my homework and practice my cello. She was a powerful presence, my mother. She would be making dinner in the kitchen, nowhere near the living room where I was sawing up and down those hellish scales, but if I missed one interval, she would call out, "No, back and do it again." I thought she heard everything, saw everything, knew everything.

And we believed in the Lord. We went to a white clapboard Swedish Baptist church, where we sang "What a Friend We Have in Jesus" and listened to long sermons calling us to forsake the vanities of this world for the surpassing joy of knowing Christ in this life and spending eternity in his bosom. It was mostly an idyllic childhood. I knew what I believed. I knew I was loved, and I had a deep sense of belonging inside the tight circle of my big family, inside that three-story Victorian house on a hill, inside the warm confines of our Swedish Baptist church.

Despite the fact that I was sent to a conservative religious college—or perhaps, finally, because of it—it was in college that I lost my puerile faith. I no longer believed in every word of the Bible. I chafed at the idea that Jesus was the only savior and that the untold millions of Asia, China, India, and Africa were all consigned to damnation and hell (except those few whom our missionaries had snatched as brands from the burning). I started attending an Episcopal church, and when my mother discovered this act of perfidy during Christmas break of my sophomore year, it ruined the holiday for everyone.

My family held out hope for me. They assumed it was an "intellectual" phase I was going through. I still felt their love, but I knew the tight circle had been broken. The years went by. I graduated from college, moved to Chicago, got married, worked painting houses to pay off my student loans, and eventually went to grad school. I had decided to become an English professor. I got my master's degree and then enrolled in a PhD program. All the while my wife, Pam, and I had found our way into a tiny Episcopal church where we sang in the choir and frequently had the eccentric vicar to our home for dinner and long conversations into the night. He was a High Church Episcopal priest who ditched the "new" Episcopal Prayer Book of the mid-1970s, used a Roman Rite on Sunday mornings, and included the "Holy Father" in Sunday prayer intentions. Our vicar, moreover, was a self-taught naturalist and early environmentalist who sipped sherry after dinner and spoke knowledgeably of botanical evolution. If my family had any idea, I thought, that my new pastor was a popish, evolutionary priest, they would stage an emergency intervention.

At annual family reunions, I shared my doubts and emerging convictions with my brothers and sisters, but we were careful to have our discussions in the basement, late at night, after Mom and Dad were in bed. Mother did not like conflict. When discussions veered off the approved track, she would get up, sigh deeply, and leave the room. That was our signal: this line of discussion is forbidden. So we held secret conclave in the basement. The conflict was painful. I was moving outside the circle. I knew it, my family knew it. Still, I felt a deep love within my cherished clan. It was alloyed with sadness and fear and regret, but it was love.

Most people who attempt a PhD spend years in purgatory, if not the inferno. My attempt was mostly purgatorial, stringing on for years. Pam and I bought a house and had our first child. I failed the oral exam and couldn't begin the dissertation-writing phase; I had to study to retake the orals. We ran low on money. I had to get a job on the side, and I began teaching literature and writing workshops at a small college in Chicago. I hardly had a free moment to study for those orals. But the truth was, the PhD was fading for me. I was spending more time reading theology and church history. I was elected to the vestry at our little church. I became a lay assistant, serving at the altar, and I started a children's choir. Everything about ministry in this new church excited me. I wanted to be a priest, but the thought was so frightening I could not even admit it to myself. It was finally the vicar who said to me one day at the altar, "You want to do this, don't you?" I claimed not to have given it much thought. "I can tell," he said, "just by watching you." *Was it that obvious?* I thought.

There were many reasons to deny any such vocation. I had spent years—racked up thousands in debt—pursuing first an MA, then a PhD. Was that all for naught? After years of grad school, it was time for me to start my career and get a real paycheck. Our second child had just been born. Pam couldn't support us forever.

Those were all good reasons, but they weren't the real barrier. That was my family, my white clapboard Baptist church, my castle-like Victorian on a hill. All of that told me who I was, what I believed, what my life's purpose was. To become a professor was an honorable profession in my family. To become a priest was not. I could not imagine telling my mother what I felt called to do. She would disown me. So would my father. Plenty of people are forced to wait until after the death of their father or mother to follow their life's vocation. I guessed that I was one of those people.

Fear kept me in the basement like that for a long time. I hid my real life and scotched my real aspirations. Then it all ended in the oddest way. I finished studying for my second shot at the oral exam. I sat before a panel of six professors, and I passed. They shook my hand, and my advisor suggested we get together soon to sketch out my dissertation. I nodded, left the university, went home, shaved my beard, and announced to my wife that I was going to seminary. The next morning I called my parents. They acknowledged that this was tough for them, but they wished me the best and asked how the two kids were doing. That was all.

We learned this lesson at the Good-Bye Gate: the first passage toward an adult soul is recognizing the whole conventional web that has you in thrall. The whole system operates on unquestioned authority. You do what "they" tell you to do, and life goes easier for you. When you're young you rely on parents, teachers, coaches, pastors, and the policeman on the corner to tell you what's right. Children and young people need this because authority figures confer a sense of security, and kids need that more than anything else. A child doesn't have to worry about moral and ethical decisions because the "big people" in their lives make all those decisions for them. That's as it should be. But as we grow older, we inevitably see the limitations of those authority figures. They don't have all the answers. In fact, most of what they offered as absolute truth was only partially true. This is the theme of every coming-of-age book or movie. The world is so much bigger, wilder, more inscrutable than they told us.

This second passage is just a bit tougher to maneuver. It moves from recognizing the situation to *doing* something about it. After reading from the approved script, you finally speak from the power and authenticity of your own experience. Stand apart.

Many adults come to this point and balk. They enter this brave new world, and it's painful and frightening, because the one thing you must leave behind is security. The authority figures are gone now. So are the old verities. You have to make your own decisions about what's right and wrong—for *you*. You have to make choices, not so much between good and evil as between one imperfect good and another. The old categories they gave you no longer hold. The unquestioned heroes are now clearly flawed, and the people they taught you to fear as the enemy turn out to have their own stories to tell. Most difficult of all, you have to take responsibility for your own life: what you will be, what you will do. You're done playing the victim, done blaming other people for why you can't live the life you say you want to live. You finally accept the fact that there's only one life you can change: your own. You forgive the people who wounded you (even though they may have been doing the best they could). Responsibility lies solely with you now. You're willing to accept the consequences of living the only life you know to be right. And there will be consequences. It's always harder to walk the narrow way.

This is where many of us turn back. We willingly give up our own authority in exchange for security because it's easier than struggling and bleeding a little for the truth. We don't challenge our parents on matters of belief or conviction. (After all, Mom and Dad are paying for Jenny to go to that private school.) Men forsake the call of their inner lives and create counterfeit selves that will assure them success and prestige. Women who are consigned to rigidly traditional roles with no hope of following their own callings refuse to challenge their husbands and demand a marriage of equals. They cower quietly, afraid of what might happen to their stable world if they simply asserted themselves. In exchange for security, we seek out authoritarian churches and hard-line political organizations—Left and Right— that promise rectitude and certitude. And in order to bolster the fragility of a wholly confected system, we join clubs and associations of the like-minded.

In other words, growing up is hard to do. One of the gifts of maturity, however, is simply this: you get tired of living someone else's life, and your youthful fears begin to ebb. One day you think, *What was I so afraid of all those years? What would really happen if I started*

telling certain emperors that they had no clothes? Nothing much, really. I
love these lines from May Sarton,

> Now I become myself. It's taken
> Time, many years and places;
> I have been dissolved and shaken,
> Worn other people's faces,
> Run madly, as if Time were there,
> Terribly old, crying a warning,
> "Hurry, you will be dead before—"[2]

This is the moment when you finally have the courage to say,
"Now I become myself." Now.

Every great spiritual odyssey begins with a line in the sand like
this. You draw a nice, clean boundary between you and the system
that formed and nurtured you. And because that forming and nurturing was a true gift, when the time comes to draw the line, you do it
with humility and gratitude. But you do it.

When his father brings him before the bishop, hoping the great
religious authority will force his son to renounce his eccentric ways,
Francis of Assisi strips naked on the steps of the cathedral and hands
his clothes to the bishop.[3] After his baptism, the Spirit drives Jesus
"into the wilderness."[4] His public ministry cannot begin until he
spends forty days and forty nights cut off from the community that
formed and nurtured him. The three great temptations he undergoes
are all meant to answer one question: Are you still Mama's boy? Jesus
cannot take anyone with him. He cannot rely on the family rabbi to
tell him what to do. There's no one out in the wilderness to call on,
and the Tempter is far too powerful. If Jesus has not internalized the
great tradition of his tribe and people—if he has only, so to speak,
memorized his lines—he will not survive this soul ordeal.

Claiming your own self is always a process of separation. Since adolescence you've been forming a self by identifying with this or that group. (If you've forgotten those days, just remember how teens travel in packs.) Family, race, clan, religion, social status, and scores of sub-groups all define a piece of who you are. Becoming yourself, then, entails a series of separations. Carl Jung called it "individuation." Psychiatrist Murray Bowen called it "differentiation of self."[5] It's what enables you to stand apart, stand on your own two feet. It's how you unhook from an unhealthy reliance on external sources of authority and begin to author yourself. It enables you to say, "I no longer believe that." "I don't choose to participate in that anymore." "That is not my calling and never was." You don't need to explain yourself to anybody; you don't need to justify your choices; you don't have to apologize to anybody for your life. You don't claim some unique status. You don't think you're anything special because you've self-differentiated. You just know who you are, and that is its own reward.

I opened this chapter with that climactic moment in *The Wizard of Oz*. Dorothy and her companions have come all this way, finally, to the only power who can fill the crippling emptiness of their lives and grant Dorothy a safe passage home. Trembling in abject terror, the four lost mortals approach the exalted throne of "God." Smoke billowing, flames leaping, voice booming. It's the classic depiction of the scary Man Upstairs, "the great and terrible Oz."

They approach, he bellows. The Scarecrow is scared of course, the Tin Man is rattled, and the Lion is soiling himself. Until Toto intervenes. His canine heart oblivious to the menacing presence of God, the little black dog notices some curious movement, wanders over, and yanks back a curtain. There, lo and behold, is a little man feverishly pulling the levers of heavenly power.

As a child watching the movie, I was crushed by the loss of "God."

Who now can save these people? But this, of course, is the moment when good things start happening. Dorothy and company discover that the Wizard God—who stands for all the frightening authority figures who haunt our lives—can be, no, must be defied. That's a terrifying thing to do, which is why so few will dare it. But when you do, you understand that only "God" has died, and a richer incarnation of the divine is now free to arise, not in flames and thunderclaps in some vast temple, but in the sanctuary of your own soul. Quite simply, to discover your self is to find God. It can hardly be otherwise, for God is ultimately the One who authors you.

When you reach this point, you don't need any other authority. It's all *in here.* The Tin Man already has a heart. The Lion has all the courage he needs. The Scarecrow has a brain—it's just a class of native intelligence he hadn't recognized. And no one can take Dorothy home since, as we realize in the moment she wakes in her own bed, she never left it.

This is what it means to stand apart. Pause here for a moment, and locate that inner authority. (There may be some wizards you must defy.) It is important that you come fully into your own sense of God-given, innate power, because you will need it for the family matters that await you now.

SIX

(Finally) Leaving Home

I will tell you what I will do and what I will not do.
I will not serve that in which I no longer believe,
whether it call itself my home, my fatherland, or my
church: and I will try to express myself in some mode
of life or art as freely as I can and as wholly as I can,
using for my defence the only arms I allow myself to
use—silence, exile and cunning.

—Stephen Dedalus, about to leave his Dublin home
for Paris in *A Portrait of the Artist as a Young Man*
by James Joyce

The day the child realizes that all adults are imperfect,
he becomes an adolescent; the day he forgives them,
he becomes an adult; the day he forgives himself, he
becomes wise.

—Alden Nowlan

The ones who give you life—who name you at birth—will try to
tell you who you are for the rest of your life. It's their idea of love
and belonging. Any attempt to claim your God-given self, then, will
always be a family matter.

"Every one of us was a *we* before we became an *I*." John Bradshaw's wisdom points up the dual quandary of family and self. You need a family to make you a *we;* then you need to separate from that family to become an *I.* The *we* part happens naturally, blindly, without your doing a thing. The *I* part—that takes a little work. Happily, nature and the life cycle conspire to force this necessary severance.

One day, everyone runs afoul of the family.* When you're young, you imagine that you alone in all the world have been singled out for such suffering. Then you hear the story of the ugly duckling. Remember? The egg hatches and everybody says, "I've never seen such an ugly creature." His mother doesn't want to take him in, and his father is embarrassed. Of course all the siblings make fun of him because he doesn't fit with them. Then one day two swans swim by, and they recognize him. Even in his awkward, half-formed cygnet state, he's handsome, attractive, he fits with them. That's because he's not a duck, he's a swan.

You hear that story as a child and it registers at some unconscious level you don't yet understand but one day will: it's normal to feel like an alien in your own family.

If you've ever wondered if you have somehow landed in the wrong family, Jungian author and master storyteller Clarissa Pinkola Estés has a word for you.

> You have feathers, they have scales. Your idea of a good time
> is the forest, the wilds, the inner life, the outer majesty. Their
> idea of a good time is folding towels. If this is so for you in
> your family, then you are a victim of the Mistaken Zygote
> Syndrome....
>   You've never heard of that? Well see, the Zygote Fairy was
> flying over your hometown one night, and all of the little zygotes
> in her basket were hopping and jumping with excitement.

---

* By "family" I almost always mean your family of origin.

You were indeed destined for parents who would have understood you, but the Zygote Fairy hit turbulence and, oops, you fell out of the basket over the wrong house. You fell head over heels, head over heels, right into a family that was not meant for you. Your "real" family was three miles farther on.

That is why you fell in love with a family that wasn't yours, and that lived three miles over. You always wished Mrs. and Mr. So-and-So were your real parents. Chances are they were meant to be.

That is why you tap-dance down the hallways even though you come from a family of television spores. This is why your parents are alarmed every time you come home or call. They worry, "What will she do next? She embarrassed us last time, God only knows what she will do now. Ai!" They cover their eyes when they see you coming and it is not because your light dazzles them.

All you want is love. All they want is peace.[1]

I love that quirky story of the Zygote Fairy because it illustrates a near-universal phenomenon. In childhood or adolescence you may believe—almost literally—that the people sleeping upstairs in the master bedroom cannot be your true parents and that the family three miles down the road would be heaven to be part of. But for me the story suggests that the process of becoming an adult always shapes us into some new being, one that the folks at home don't recognize as "our own" anymore. Even if you don't feel you've wandered beyond the pale, they do. *Whatever happened to our wonderful son or daughter?* they seem to ask. The answer to that plangent question is simply, she grew up and became a woman. He grew up and became a man. Yet the people in the master bedroom can never quite understand how this happens. They don't know how to *be* a parent to this new being, and—the way the world works—it often falls to the adult child to show them. You could hope that the ones who were always older and more experienced would be the ones to show the way—help you, and them, to find a new basis of relationship: parent to *adult* child. But life is not usually so kind. Some lucky souls have parents who recognize this transition, try on a new role, and give the adult child plenty of room to grow. Most of us, unfortunately, have to take the initiative on this. We must be the ones to break the old pattern (where pain is inevitable) and declare new terms of engagement.

Kim is a dramatic, humorous case in point.

"I was an only child, growing up in the South," she said as she told her story to the group on retreat. "I was totally boxed in. My parents controlled everything. They were terrified that something would happen to me. They wanted my life to be smooth and trouble-free and just perfect. Well, that didn't help me, because after I grew up and began to have problems, my parents were no help to me. After all, I could *have* no problems.

"When I graduated college, I was supposed to go to grad school, but I became a flight attendant just to get away from them. The first flight I worked flew to Pamplona, Spain. I ran with the bulls, like Hemingway." We all gasped then laughed. She said, "A nice elderly Spanish man pulled me out of it before I could be in any harm's way."

Sometimes a nice southern girl, raised in a bubble of faux safety, must flee to Pamplona and run with the bulls, if that's what it takes to break the old ties and stake claim to a new, adult identity.

It may seem odd that in a book on spiritual growth we should devote a chapter to your family. Isn't that more psychology than spirituality? No, actually. Growing a deeply wise soul is a gestational process, and one of the earliest stages in that formation is the firming up of a separate self. No one can do this without severing family ties. That may sound selfish or even cruel, but trust your soul's gestation. The separate self that must emerge is only provisional. The goal is ultimately to give your self away, to come into union with God and with all people—your family included. But the way this works, healthy separation must precede blissful union.

⸺

In the last chapter we began this important work of self-differentiation. The work we now do inside the bonds of family is the next important step in this process.

As we discovered in chapter 4, the issue we face here is mostly a problem of love that cannot let go at the border between one life stage and the next. Every child, every young person needs a strong family who can, in Bradshaw's terms, make you a *we.* What begins as a blessing, though, in time grows malignant. Just when you need to become your own *I,* the embrace of the tight circle becomes a possessive clutching. Now the gift of belonging inside the group becomes groupthink. The will and soul of the clan come to substitute for your own will, your own soul, and many are not even aware of this.

This isn't a blame game, however. Unless you were abused, there's nothing really wrong with your family. Good families hold on to their own (I've seen families who don't care enough to hold on, and it's no blessing). It's just that loving families tend to cling a little too long. Far from blaming the family, this path leads ultimately to a powerful forgiveness (see chapter 17). But first the separation.

Murray Bowen, the psychiatrist who in the 1950s developed the theory of family systems, describes the average family as an "undifferentiated ego mass,"[2] where kindred members are emotionally fused. They depend on other people's approval or acceptance. No one wants to rock the boat. Without saying a word, the dominant figures in the system insist on conformity from everyone in the family, and from early childhood people learn to fall in line.

If that compliance ended the moment we left home for college or the army, it would be all right. But you can be forty-five with children of your own and a high-level job managing a team of seventy people…until you go home for Thanksgiving. Then suddenly, a weird dynamic descends. You might as well be thirteen again. You find yourself relating to your parents and siblings as a dependent child would. The family system quashes your thoughts, opinions, and actions—and you decide it's better not to put up a fight. The only way to become your adult self, Bowen advises, is to become unfused, to differentiate yourself from that undifferentiated ego mass.

It's not enough, though, simply to choose the opposite of your family's preference. That is nothing more than adolescent rebellion. The spiritual work of becoming an *adult* child means discerning the shape and content of your unique inner life, and not fearing to give it expression. Once you take this step, you really leave home for the first time. This doesn't mean abandoning your family of origin, however. It doesn't mean disrespecting or dishonoring your parents. Rather, it's an acknowledgment that they are free to stand apart, just as you are.

When Dan and I met to talk about a new project he was helping to lead, he mentioned in passing that he was a little stressed out. When I asked what was ratcheting up his stress level, he told me that his parents were coming for a visit. It was still a week away, and already he was popping Prilosec. The problem, Dan explained, was that his parents were very controlling and judgmental. They criticized the way he and his wife raised their two boys. They made joking comments about his social and political views, but the levity was a light veil thrown over massive judgment. They drank a little too much, and when his mother was over-oiled she would scold the children, frightening them.

"Don't misunderstand," Dan said. "We're a close family. I'm the eldest child, and my dad raised me to excel." But the prospect of their visit had him making secret plans. They were going to ask some friends to just "drop by" around dinnertime one night, hoping the presence of outsiders would break up the typical family pattern of "concerned" criticism that always led to argument. Dan and his wife found themselves coaching the children on how to answer certain questions that Grandma and Grandpa might ask.

I listened to all these preparations and said, "Dan, the only question is, Do you want to have an adult relationship with your parents?" He was stunned, silent. Dan knew exactly what I meant. If he related to them as peers, he wouldn't be making these contortionist plans to accommodate two bullies! He would speak the truth and be himself. He couldn't imagine doing that; in fact, he confessed that he had never once considered it.

Dan's situation is not unusual. In fact, most adults are enmeshed in relationships born years ago in that undifferentiated ego mass, mostly with Mom and Dad. Some are actually dominated by their parents. The idea of being open with your parents, your siblings, your aunts and uncles, and all the characters who walk the main street of your hometown—the idea of being your adult self—is considered too risky.

People typically justify living a false life in front of their parents either because they fear disapproval and some kind of emotional backlash, or because they want to "protect" their parents. "They're too old to change now. It's not worth it. I don't want to hurt them." You want the emotional closeness of your family of origin for your kids—your parents' grandkids—but you sense that the only way to preserve that is to go along with the family and to act like someone you're really not anymore. You can't imagine a separation that leads, in fact, to a closer, more intimate and real relationship.

Many people who insist on living into their separate, adult selves manage to do so only by rejecting their family of origin and living in either virtual or actual estrangement. What I want to show you is this beautiful mystery: the way to a real and fulfilling relationship with your family is to separate from them so that you can enter into a new rapport as peers. In other words, what is good and right for you turns out to bless and enable them—if they choose—to come into new selves as well. I called this mystery beautiful, but it is also difficult. It can be painful. It can take years. Sometimes the family doesn't respond well. But like any other experience of reality, once you see and know it, you would not trade it for a part-time counterfeit life.

The work I am laying out for you is deeply spiritual, not simply therapeutic. That is, it's not about developing a better relationship with the folks back home and avoiding the family atrocities that ruin otherwise lovely holidays (though these are likely by-products of this work). If you are going to find your soul, you must first lay hold of your actual self, draw it out from the undifferentiated ego mass, sequester it alone.

An important note here: Because they are the stuff of archetype, myth, and legend, Mother and Father have been our primary focus. But you may feel dominated by a powerful sibling who has always put you in your place. An overbearing aunt or uncle can hold you in a mysterious way, even after you are all grown up with a family of your own. And marriages often become relational quicksand, holding spouses in outgrown roles and preventing them from becoming new—and different!—people. These are all classic snares in which your divinely ordained self can be trapped. Now is the moment to stand apart. You can read books on spirituality and go on endless retreats, but the real work of finding your soul waits upon this courageous and liberating act.

In sum, then, we know two things. Your family represents a threat to your personal and spiritual growth, *and* there's nothing wrong with your family. If you grasp only the first truth, you are likely to be a selfish child (no matter your age), angry at your parents and siblings (or your spouse or partner) for causing all your problems. You will resent that your family treats you like a child, forgetting that the act of self-differentiation as an adult can be initiated only by you. Only deeply mature people are able and ready to acknowledge both of these truths together.

To accept the second—that there's nothing wrong with your family—is to be humble. It is to forgive those we love and who love us, recognizing the weakness and selfishness in all human love. It is to acknowledge that as mothers and fathers we have recapitulated with our own children the very acts of coercion we so deplore in our parents. But if you can make that double assent, you are ready to be an adult child.

The arc of leave-taking eventually curves back to a homecoming, but that comes later. First comes the work of separation. To do this you have to move beyond sentimental notions of the family and understand its powers both to bless and to oppress, to mother and to smother. This is the truth about every family, even good families where the bonds are stronger inside that ego mass. When you realize that the dark side of your family is only the shadow of its light—that the two are always and everywhere one—your parting doesn't have to be angry or fearful or dripping with blame. You just know your situation is painfully, comically universal. You know what you need to do.

All the great religious traditions have understood the spiritual power hidden in the family and how each man or woman must engage it. After Muhammad received from Allah the charge to form a new community of God's people, the *ummah* was born.[3] The *ummah* is for Muslims what the body of Christ is for Christians: a unified community that transcends geographical, cultural, tribal, and ethnic boundaries.

In 622, Arab families who converted to Islam slipped out of Mecca and began the migration (Hijra) to Medina, the center of this new faith community. They canceled old blood feuds and vowed to live in peace with former enemies. In this fiercely tribal culture, however, the families they left behind were not impressed with such irenic ideals. Any new community that entailed leaving your family was inherently wrong.[4]

"In pre-Islamic Arabia," Karen Armstrong writes in *Islam: A Short History*, "the tribe was a sacred value. To turn your back on your blood-group and join another was unheard of; it was essentially blasphemous, and the [leaders of Mecca] could not condone this defection. They vowed to exterminate the *ummah* in Yathrib. Muhammad had become the head of a collection of tribal groups that were not bound together by blood but by a shared ideology, an astonishing innovation in Arabian society."[5]

Every Christian has squirmed in the pew at hearing Jesus's words, "Whoever comes to me and does not hate father and mother, wife and children, brothers and sisters, yes, and even life itself, cannot be my disciple."[6] Inevitably the preacher quiets our squirming with a brief disquisition on the use of hyperbole in the ancient Near East. Not to worry, we are told; all this scary gospel means is, you must love God so much that, by comparison, all other human loves are as hatred.

That reading will get you through the first few decades, but later in life you start to hear the soul rumble of Jesus's words. You know the power of the family to enfold and bless a child, but you can also *feel* the power of the family system to bind each member in his appointed place. It is subtle and often benevolent, but it is coercive.

A good friend told me a few years ago about a recent family gathering. "The whole family was home for a bar mitzvah," Helen said, "and my older sister—she's fifty-one—is there. She decides that she doesn't have the right shoes for the ceremony so she goes shopping for a new pair. Patty comes home with her new shoes, takes them out of the box, and puts them on. My mother takes one look and says, 'In this family we don't wear *red* shoes.'" Helen is laughing, and I am shaking my head. Patty is fifty-one, and her mother is bent on controlling her shoe color as if she were five.

That is the coercive power Jesus is naming when he calls for hatred. It's a subtle subversion of our own personal authority. Helen's family is quite close and healthy in many ways. Her mother is hardly a harridan. It's just the way all families operate, even good ones.

It's almost humorous when the shoe color you prefer does not pass muster back home. It's not so funny when the fiancé you choose, the church you prefer, or the career you embrace fails the test of home. These are the life choices that reveal a person's emerging, actual self, and making these choices fearlessly is how we differentiate from the family. If you have ever attempted such choices, however, you know that for every separating action there is an equal and opposite *reaction*. The family pulls back. The undifferentiated ego mass only works when everyone stays in her appointed role. When one person breaks out, it throws the mass into a tizzy. The unconscious response, then, is to pull the separate person back.

People who live in an alcoholic home know a lot about this pullback. If you name the family sickness, there will be anger and accusation. There will be tears and all kinds of emotional turmoil. The innocent, suffering people in the family will ask you to stop—stop causing such trouble in the family. But if you make nice and settle back into your well-worn spot in the system, everyone will breathe a sigh of relief. The system always pulls back to stasis, which is why lasting change is always doggedly hard work.

If, however, you can stand apart and *stay apart,* two blessed things begin to happen: you lay hold of your actual God-given self, and everyone inside the family system is empowered for healing, freedom, and grace. The key is to withstand the initial pullback—and all its emotional fireworks. When you know it's coming, you don't take it personally. You understand it's an unconscious, systemic response.

This happens in all families, even the holy family. Once, Mark's gospel tells us, Jesus entered a house, and an enormous crowd overwhelmed the place "so that he and his disciples were not even able to eat." The energy of the Jesus movement is swirling, drawing in a strange congeries of people, men of all classes, people with diseases that rendered them untouchable, people with mental illnesses—and *women*! Mark says, "When his family heard about this, they went to take charge of him, for they said, 'He is out of his mind.'" So they come for him. They stand outside the crush of people, disdainful of this crazy mosh pit. Finally someone inside yells, "Your mother and brothers are outside looking for you." Jesus replies, "'Who are my mother and my brothers?'... Then he looked at those seated in a circle around him and said, 'Here are my mother and my brothers! Whoever does God's will is my brother and sister and mother.'"[7]

The message is uncomfortably clear. If you stand apart from your family and do God's will *as only you can do,* the home folks will think you are out of your mind. And they will come for you. They do it in love, hoping to save you from making a bad end (they are so afraid of the unknown and the different, of embarrassment and dishonor). They will want to take you home where you can get a shower, a hot meal, and a warm bed. In the morning, certainly, you will return to your right mind and to your appointed place in the family system.

Jesus models clearly for us how to stand apart from a loving family, in order to live fully into the divine calling that rests upon every man and woman. If Jesus had tried to be a more "loving" son and brother, he would have forfeited his vocation. That's why I put strong emphasis here on the family. This work of separating the self from the family system is on the critical path to an adult soul.

Sarah sat in my office one winter afternoon. I offered her a cup of tea; she sipped Earl Grey and unloaded. It was not one thing. It was a host of small things adding up. Sarah was in her early fifties, a successful photographer whose work had appeared in some of the finest magazines. But now she was "stuck," as she put it. Creatively stymied. In the past ten years she had put on maybe thirty pounds. She didn't feel good; she had no energy. Her son was in Brazil for his junior year abroad, and her daughter had left for college in the fall. The house was empty. Her husband had recently taken a new job, and since the kids were gone and she was busy, he stayed late at the office. Sarah would make dinner and wait for Allen to come home, drinking red wine with one eye on the clock. There were no big fights, Sarah mused, it was just slightly distant. When Allen wrote major reports, Sarah read them, commented, offered changes. But he could walk past a table covered with her photos and never ask what she was up to. They had sex occasionally, but Allen was "somewhere else" emotionally.

When Sarah told a friend that she had failed at her third diet in six months, the woman recommended a therapist.

"She's helping me," Sarah said with a tired smile, "but we're not talking about french fries. She suggested I may be carrying extra weight because I'm carrying heavy burdens—doing more for people than I should, taking care of everyone except myself." Sarah couldn't take care of herself because she didn't actually know who she was. That was the problem. She'd been a good girl growing up, then a good wife, a good mother. She'd done well professionally, brought home more bacon than Allen. Yet he acted like the lord of the manor, and she felt like the slave girl. "I don't think I've ever lived my own life," she said.

A few months passed, and Sarah came by for another talk.

"You've lost weight," I said.

"And I'm not dieting," she said. "What I'm shedding are all the things other people have been putting on me—and I've just carried them."

She had started with Allen. "I demanded his love," she said matter-of-factly. "I'm giving my love, and I'm too good to settle for less from him. I told him if he couldn't give that, then I was done."

It was working. Things were changing. But the next challenge was even more daunting: her mother and father.

Sarah was about to go home to visit her parents in North Carolina. She could predict the whole ghastly weekend. For years her parents would comment on political, social, and religious issues as if, of course, everyone at the table shared the same viewpoint. Sarah could always be counted on to keep quiet. Always the good girl. You don't sass your elders. "I just go down there and bite my tongue." When I asked why she didn't speak up and share her own thoughts and opinions, she recalled family feuds and all the aunts and uncles who were not welcome in her childhood home because of some petty argument ten years earlier. "I'm worried that my mother will cut me off. And there go my kids' grandparents."

Even though she was worried, Sarah was ready. She had taken the first self-defining step with her husband, and she could feel the difference it was making in her life. She knew what she had to do with her parents.

The time came for her annual trip, but this time Sarah prepared. She imagined the situations when she was likely to be coerced into the silence of assumed consent, and she prepared not simply her verbal but her emotional responses. This time, when parental opinions were offered as universal truths, Sarah said simply, without emotion, "Actually, I don't share that opinion, and I haven't for thirty years." When her mother insisted they take their usual shopping excursion— a dreaded experience in which her mother unfailingly declared the latest fashions scandalous and the sale items overpriced—Sarah just said, "Oh, not this time, Mom, you go on. I think I'll just sit in the sun and read my book." In a quiet moment with her father, Sarah named a pink elephant. Her cousin Barbara was a lesbian. Most everybody knew it, yet her parents frequently wondered aloud "when Barbie's going to get married."

"Dad," Sarah said, "you know Barbara's a lesbian, don't you?" Her father shrugged and nodded simultaneously. "I just wanted to say that—so we don't have to pretend about it. Okay?"

That led to a long, honest talk. It went on like that all weekend. It was awkward at times, but Sarah felt a calm empowerment and a peace she could hardly believe.

"I just wonder," she said to me, "why it took me so long."

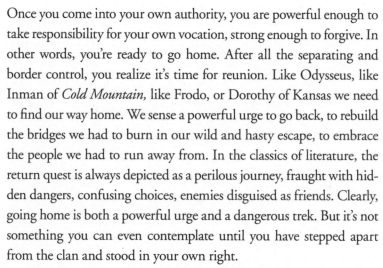

Once you come into your own authority, you are powerful enough to take responsibility for your own vocation, strong enough to forgive. In other words, you're ready to go home. After all the separating and border control, you realize it's time for reunion. Like Odysseus, like Inman of *Cold Mountain,* like Frodo, or Dorothy of Kansas we need to find our way home. We sense a powerful urge to go back, to rebuild the bridges we had to burn in our wild and hasty escape, to embrace the people we had to run away from. In the classics of literature, the return quest is always depicted as a perilous journey, fraught with hidden dangers, confusing choices, enemies disguised as friends. Clearly, going home is both a powerful urge and a dangerous trek. But it's not something you can even contemplate until you have stepped apart from the clan and stood in your own right.

It is the soul's paradox: only those who have left home can truly go home. Trust that everlasting pattern. In the beginning you will likely be misunderstood, scolded, or questioned. Homecoming will seem a sad impossibility. I promise, though, that you will get there even if the people who live at that old address never fully understand or accept or embrace you. If, like Jesus, you can stand in your own right and *stay there* in love and compassion, you will know who you are and where you belong. You will be home, even if others are slow to join you there. Still, the persistent miracle is how often one person's courageous self-differentiation offers health and blessing to the whole system, bringing everyone into a new experience of family and home.

We're peeking over the Jordan now, into the Promised Land. What you will find as you do the early work of separation, firming up the core of your own being, is that you are no longer dependent on other people to change so that you can change. You don't need them to be less controlling so that you can be free, to be less depressing so that you can be happy, or to act like a mature adult so that you can too. You start to find your own authority, your own power. You are able to forgive others and release them—so that you can love them again.

But we're not in Canaan yet. It's important first to locate your own authentic self and to cut the unhealthy ties that bind. Do not try to go back if you've never actually left. Do not try to embrace or forgive when you haven't had the courage to step away and say, "That's not me. Not anymore." Otherwise the going back is recidivist, the embrace is false, and the forgiveness has no transforming power.

Many people have been taught that it is selfish to be yourself and that we love people by being what they need us to be. I give you, therefore, explicit permission to do this. Stand apart.

SEVEN

It's Not About Being Good Anymore

Now is the time to understand
That all your ideas of right and wrong
Were just a child's training wheels
To be laid aside
When you can finally live
With veracity
And love.

     —Hafiz

People say we need religion, when what they really
mean is we need police.

     —H. L. Mencken

In the winter of 2000 I was in trouble. The backstory you already know. The church I was serving had burned down a year and a half earlier, and the stress of holding together a community in crisis was grinding me down. Two cherished friends had died, one in her sleep, the other after a long battle with prostate cancer. Then my mother died.

My relationship to Mom was complicated. I loved her, but I did not really know her. When the doctor told my mother that the stomach pains she complained of were actually pancreatic cancer, she refused any treatment and took to her bed. She grieved privately. When my siblings and I called to say we were coming to visit, she said (through my father) that she wasn't up for it. "Later." We should come later. We honored her wishes at first, but then we went anyway. In four months she was dead, along with any hopes I had of some deeper understanding.

That's when I slid into depression. I wish I could say that my way of being depressed was to pull the covers over my head or to drink a little too much and get weepy. Instead, my way was to feel sorry for myself. Work was my ticket to success, and since I could not manage it all, I was exhausted and resentful of people who weren't working as hard as I was. At the end of the day, I went home with nothing to give my wife, Pam, and our two teenage daughters. I pitied myself, stared at my wounds. The usual marital tiffs turned into longer, more bitter fights. Mostly I responded with silence and scorn. One night at the dinner table the afternoon's battle erupted again over spaghetti. I said some cruel things to Pam that startled my daughters—it was ugly. I was ashamed and did what men often do. I walked out of the house and didn't come back until after midnight.

I remember crawling into bed in the darkness and hearing Pam breathing. It was the respiration of a woman fully awake. Somewhere deep in the night she spoke. It was time for me to get help or get gone.

The next morning, as it happened, I was scheduled to get gone. My oldest friend from high school was coming out from St. Louis to spend a long weekend with me, a get-together we had planned months ago. We were going to Cape May, New Jersey, to walk the shore, to have a few quiet dinners, see a few movies, talk.

When Tom arrived, he sensed the awkwardness in our home. I packed a bag and left. We got in the car, and I pretended to have fun, like old times. But inside I felt sick. I'm pretty sure women would have talked about a mess like mine. Either I would have confided in Tom, or he would have asked me to talk about what was so obviously not right. But neither of us said anything. On our second night, I left the restaurant where we were having dinner to call home. It was a difficult phone call; Pam now speaking of divorce. When I came back to the table, Tom asked how things were at home. I told him "not so good."

"Look," Tom said with real kindness, "if you need to go home, we don't have to stay here. I understand."

I felt embarrassed, ashamed. We had planned this trip with such eagerness. Tom had come all the way from St. Louis, and my problems were like a contagious disease.

"I'm sorry," I said. "Things are pretty bad for me right now at home, with Pam. I'm in trouble and I don't know how I got here exactly and I don't know how to get out of it alive."

I didn't say it, but I felt even worse about my daughters. They were fifteen and seventeen, just old enough to sense real, adult crisis. Old enough to understand that their father was a jerk. Their *minister* father was selfish and small-minded and pathetic.

Tom nodded and said, "It's okay."

"I'm just sorry I've brought you into this whole mess," I said. "You come all the way out here for a great weekend, and all my problems have ruined the whole thing. I apologize—" Tom cut me off.

"Please don't apologize," he said firmly. "I'm your friend. The point was to have a long weekend together, and you haven't ruined anything for me." Tom paused, and then he said something that would have shocked me if I hadn't known Tom—and his flat-out candor—for twenty-eight years. "Actually," he said, "I like you better this way."

The book of Proverbs says, "Wounds from a friend can be trusted."[1] Tom had taken an ice pick and driven it deep enough to puncture my ego. Here I was pretending to be fine when any fool could see I was gutted. And then I had to apologize—as if I had offended a lifelong friend by having a problem in his presence, and (this is what really torqued him) as if I were somehow responsible to see that Tom's weekend was perfect. His wounding words were just what I needed. I was struck dumb. Tom flashed a half-smile that said, *You can stop being a pompous ass now. It's okay if you're in deep caca. I can handle it. I'm your friend. Remember?*

———

The most important thing I can say about spiritual development is that it's not about being good anymore.

In order to make this second passage and stand apart, you must exorcise your angels. The moral vision that drives conventional faith is all about goodness, or at least the appearance of goodness, and here is where you part ways. This is actually a two-stage separation. The first is external, the second is internal.

The first separation is from the external sources of authority that define the terms of moral goodness and police its boundaries. In short, it's the end of being good to please those in authority and qualify for their approbation.

The second separation is a little dicier. It is a separation from your own ego, which loves the notion of being an exclusively good person and wants you to spend your whole life pretending to be that shining illusion. In short, it's the end of the Do-It-Yourself salvation project.

We begin with the first separation, the external one.

Early-stage religion is always concerned with moral purity and the disciplined eradication of our character flaws. There is a heavy emphasis on getting clean ("cleanliness is next to godliness"), of avoiding things considered dirty. It goes heavy on rules and relies on shame and guilt to enforce the code. All of this is embodied in the conventional faith that boils down to: Be a good person. Obey your parents. Listen to your teacher. Respect your elders. (My father, who fought in

World War II, taught me to address police, firemen, park rangers, anyone in uniform as "sir.") Do not lie, cheat, or steal, and do not tolerate those who do. Be kind to your little sister. Don't touch yourself there. Wash behind your ears.

Once you pass puberty, all the concern for purity and cleanliness centers on the body, and sex becomes the major battleground of morality. Other sins of the body—addictions or struggles with food, alcohol, drugs—fill out the Most Wanted list of conventional morality. But sex always tops the list. The moral standard at this early stage is almost completely externalized. It focuses on actions that can, for the most part, be seen and tallied. The mentality is either/or, all or nothing. Either you refrained from illicit sex or you didn't. Either you told the truth or you didn't. And if you failed, if you sinned, your penance is simple. Feel bad about yourself and what you have done (if you need help in this department, the authorities are happy to oblige), and then resolve even more firmly not to do it again.

This is the basic morality package of conventional faith. You might imagine that sophisticated adults these days are hardly concerned with this juvenile sort of morality, but of all the seekers I meet, nearly everybody believes that to be more spiritual means being a better person, someone who is good and who does good for others.

I think of the man I invited to serve as a lay assistant at the altar. He blanched. "I'm not good enough to be up there," he said. When I explained that if being good were the requirement, then I could not serve, he tentatively agreed.

Many people carry heavy burdens of guilt and shame for things they have done or failed to do—or for things that were done to them, over which they had no power. They believe, sadly, that they are simply not good enough for "God"—however that being is imagined. I recall the woman who came to talk with me about the frustrations of her spiritual journey and why she'd finally given up trying. "Even on my best days," she sighed, "I couldn't be good enough."

So we have to say it forcefully: it's not about being good anymore.

What we're rejecting here is moralism. For centuries, religious teachers and philosophers have offered moral codes for human behavior. Whether it is Moses giving his people the tablets of the law, or Aristotle's *Nicomachean Ethics,* the purpose of morality is to guide men and women into a life of happiness or excellence, to help them live the best lives possible. That's morality (even if the moralizers have almost ruined the word beyond reclamation). But moral*ism* is different. Moralism is following a set of rules not for some greater good, like human happiness, but for the sake of the rules themselves. Not because if you don't you won't be happy, but because if you don't you won't be accepted or loved. You'll be shamed by your family or tribe. You'll be punished.

Many families operate like this, and we have to say, ruefully, that many churches do too. We got the message almost in utero: be good, or else. It wasn't enough that Mom and Dad wanted us to be good— *God* insisted on our righteousness. People often joke with me that God would strike them with a bolt of lightning if they came into church, or that the place would simply collapse. It would be a flagrant act of defiance for an "unholy" person to enter a "holy" place. One Roman Catholic woman recalled how as a young girl she was terrified of going to hell because she ate one of her own boogers before receiving the sacrament of Holy Communion. You can't make this stuff up.

And it's not just some silly rubes who feel this way. I once heard the former secretary of state Madeleine Albright speak at a seminary. She was there because she had just written *The Mighty and the Almighty.* I almost could have predicted it. Looking out at all these clergy-types, she began with a caveat. "I do not know more about religion than anybody else. I am neither a theologian, nor quite frankly, well-enough behaved to lecture others about the nature of God."[2] It's a good laugh line because it invokes the old canard that anyone interested in the nature of God must be well-enough behaved. As annoying as I find such comments, the popular form of every religion always lives at this jejune level. The comedian Cathy Ladman is not far wrong when she remarks, "All religions are the same: religion is basically guilt with different holidays."[3]

We have all lived under the thumb of moralism. It's the darling of conventionalism. It emphasizes rules and laws and seeks external compliance. The Rule Giver is revered and so are the earthly enforcers. In the last chapter we stressed the importance of breaking with external sources of authority, and the powerful shift to your own inner sense of identity and authority—becoming your Self. You leave behind the passive-dependent phase, where other, more "important" people determine the "appropriate" role for you and set the mark for acceptable behavior. The same dynamic is at work here. At some point you have to recognize that being good to please other people—"God," your mother, your father, the church, the people at the home office— is not good. Not for you. Not now.

By now someone is surely wondering how I can be guiding people into spiritual maturity by abjuring goodness. In order to make this midfaith journey, you must be willing to descend into paradox. You must hold together two apparently contradictory truths: being good is critical in the first half of life, and *not* being good is critical in the second. Now we are undertaking that second, internal separation that requires a nuanced understanding of inner light and inner shadow.

Remember in chapter 4 the tower we must build in our early years, and the later descent we must all make? Where morality is concerned, we could say, "The task of the first half of life is to build a tower of goodness, and the task of the second half of life is to come down from your tower." But now we have to figure out how to do this. *If I descend that tower, won't I become immoral?* Hold that question for a moment.

The paradox is, you *need* to build that tower of goodness! Because human life is naturally selfish and ungoverned, children must learn the rules and discipline themselves to live within limits. It's quite obvious: unless young people learn some kind of impulse control, they fall into turbulent chaos. Without a basic sense of right and wrong, we devolve into pandemonium, harming ourselves and injuring others. That's the gift of morality. You need it, I need it. We sure don't want to live in a society without it. (When law and order breaks down and ordinary people start looting and pillaging, we shudder in fear.) So you have to build that tower of virtue; otherwise, your only option is to roam the world as a wolf.

This is where the paradox thickens. Conventional morality is *necessary*. You have to win that merit badge. And then...the time comes when you have to unpin that silly badge, turn it over in your palm, and smile at how seriously you took it. *As if that hunk of tin really made me good!*

Taking off that merit badge—making that second, internal separation—requires an understanding of your ego and the shadowy role it plays. The ego is the part of you that wants to control everything, to maintain the appearance of perfection. It's the grand impresario of the self—it needs to stage everything so that you look good, successful. In arguments, you must be right. Your religion is the true faith, your country is number one, your ethnic heritage is the crown of humanity. You are intelligent or compassionate or both. The ego acts as a gatekeeper. It allows in only those facts or opinions that bolster and support this one-sided view of your self. All other data is disallowed, shunted into the spam folder.

We all do this: welcome every shining fact that agrees with our sterling self, and deny every shred of evidence to the contrary. When someone accuses you, say, of being selfish, alarms sound and red lights start flashing on your inner control board. The egoic self is being assailed! Unless this attack can be parried, the preferred version of your self may not survive. This is where your hero always comes through. Immediately the ego supplies you with four instances in which you were manifestly selfless. You face your accuser, adduce these four facts, and triumph gloriously. The red lights stop flashing, and the blaring alarms cease. You breathe a sigh of relief. Thank God, the approved version of your self has been saved.

Unless you are aware of this basic ego struggle that roils in every human being, you will always remain in that childish phase of morality. You will lack the capacity not to fight that accusation but to welcome it: *Yes, I am selfish. I can also be selfless, but I am both.* You won't develop the deep, paradoxical sense that you are—like every human being—a wild admixture of light and darkness, good and evil. You'll keep locating darkness and evil outside your self (the ego insists vigorously on this). Way into your adult years you'll still be living in that passive-dependent phase, seeking approval and affirmation from somebody else, keeping your nose clean, attacking anyone who points out your faults, demonizing people who don't (like you) live up to the one true code of conduct. In short, you will be a Boy Scout or a Girl Scout. You know people like this? Men and women in their sixties or seventies who are still little boys, little girls, still wearing those merit badges. They aren't wise. They have learned how to be good; they have kept the rules and, by God, so should you and everybody else. They are so proud of their own rightness. They haven't acknowledged that the ego is there, much less confronted it and pulled the plug on its power.

These people are the Pharisees who are forever doing battle with Jesus. They are truly good people—I mean scary-good people who hold themselves to incredibly high standards. And yet Jesus savages these extremely religious, frightfully righteous people because they have totally mastered the conventional code of conduct—nailed it!— and yet they have never pulled back the curtain on the ego. Of course Jesus didn't use that Freudian language. He put it this way: "Why do you see the speck in your neighbor's eye, but do not notice the log in your own eye?"[4]

Spiritual maturity, the kind befitting adults and not children, means noticing the log that is in your own eye—*and not trying to get rid of it.* That's what the ego wants more than anything else, to save that image of "log less" perfection. The authorities are knocking on the door, and the ego is running around, gathering up all the incriminating evidence, flushing it down the toilet.

After we grow up, we don't have to worry about that anymore. We know we have a great big log in our eye. It's just part of our human nature. We're not perfect—we weren't created that way. To be human is to be flawed, broken in places. The creation stories of Genesis depict humans as nearly divine, made in the "image" and "likeness" of God, and yet as inherently misdirected. Adam and Eve cannot live simply knowing God and the good; they reach out and taste the fruit of the "tree of the knowledge of good and evil."[5]

Why people who knew only good could not resist evil is a mystery. In fact, it is the mystery at the heart of humanity. We are both good and evil, the great tale is telling us. That is what it means to be human. The Fall was the dawning of full human consciousness, the capacity to know both delight and sorrow, ecstasy and agony, life and death—all as one; to understand that our profoundest joys are always touched with shadow. If you have ever been deeply moved by an autumn scene of rapturous beauty in decay, you know this mystery. A child cannot know this, and once an adult has "fallen" into this mystery, that person will never go back into innocence.

That is why you have a log in your eye, and that is why you must not rush to rid yourself of it. That would only make it worse. But if you can acknowledge the log that makes you selfish and vindictive and insecure and controlling, you are on your way to salvation. The mystery is, if you can just let it be and not have to fix this or correct that or banish that, Someone else can take it from you and hold it safely on your behalf. If that makes your head swim, just stay with me: the chapters that follow all flow deeper into this holy riddle.

I did not go home that night, as Tom suggested I could. We stayed, ordered another glass of wine, and I began talking. Tom's ego-puncturing wound was truly a coup de grâce. I started to tell my best friend the truth. Actually, I couldn't quite bring myself to tell him the whole truth for another few months, but I began that night to tell one other human being how wretched and afraid I felt, and instead of feeling worse, I felt better. This is the mystery I promised you a moment ago. I did not feel better because I rose higher but because I sank lower, not because I triumphed but because I failed. It felt good to be simply a log-eyed human being, under no pressure to be something "better."

I have never forgotten Tom's words: *"I like you better this way."* Of course he did. Despite our need to appear perfect, flawless, we all prefer other people plain. Plain old human beings. I keep forgetting it, but that night I knew: it's not about being good anymore.

EIGHT

Forget Heaven & Hell (For Now)

There are people who pray for eternal life and don't
know what to do with themselves on a rainy Sunday.

—G. K. Chesterton

For those of us who believe in physics, this separation
between past, present, and future is only an illusion,
however tenacious.

—Albert Einstein

I once visited a man in the hospital. He was in his late seventies, and
this was not his first health crisis. In fact, the doctors were telling
him, it was likely his last. It had all happened so fast. Hal was a man
of the world, had lived most of his life in New York City. He came to
church occasionally, but I tended to meet Hal more often at cocktail
or dinner parties where he was clearly the bon vivant. He was a racon-
teur, a joker. (At his funeral all the men wore red clown noses during
the eulogy.)

I pulled up a chair by Hal's bed. He made a feeble attempt at
lighthearted banter, but our talk turned inevitably to his condition.
He said to me, half-joking, "So, do you think I'm going to make it?"
Though I thought he meant "heaven," I could not be sure if he meant,

"Do you think I will recover and live?" so I asked him, "What do you mean?"

Hal said with an impish smile, "Heaven. Am I going to make it to heaven? Is God going to let me in?"

I said, "What do *you* think?"

Hal said, "Oh—I don't know. I've tried to live a good life. I've done the best I can."

The twentieth-century theologian Paul Tillich suggested that we stop using the word *God* for at least a hundred years because it is so loaded with misconceptions, so fraught with emotional history. The same goes for the fused concepts, Heaven & Hell. The next passage to an adult soul requires a large black plastic trash bag. I want you to take everything you believe about Heaven & Hell, everything you love about those words, everything you hate, and put it into that black bag now. This means you. Even if you think you're plenty liberal and don't believe in a literal version of those eternal destinations: into the black plastic bag. Now we twist the top of the bag, tie a big knot, and walk the bag to the nearest metaphysical Dumpster.

You must dispose of Heaven & Hell for two reasons.

First, because (in terms of the last chapter) it is the ultimate moralism, enforced by the ultimate external authority. The whole construct of an afterlife divided cleanly into brimstone or bliss is built on the moralizing model: the same judgments that control everyday life are now projected into eternity. Once you begin to claim your own inner authority, however—once you're onto the ego's obsession with being good—you won't be able to get to that Dumpster fast enough. It's a stand-apart moment. You step away from *the* central tenet of conventional faith.

Hal's story illustrates the dominant notion of Heaven & Hell. Hal was sure that trying to live a good life—doing the best you can—is the critical issue. From the time we are children, we understand that the system rewards us when we are good and punishes us when we are bad. (Which led to Helen Gurley Brown's quip, "Good girls go to heaven, bad girls go everywhere."[1]) But Hal also knew that this same issue of personal goodness determined the destiny of his immortal soul in the life of the world to come. No matter how much some spiritual leaders preach grace and mercy, unconditional love and forgiveness, people like Hal "know" better. Despite the culture's drumbeat of self-esteem, we all battle demons of guilt and shame. Sermons from childhood—like Father Arnall's infamous sermon on the hideous torture of hell, visited on a poor class of young Catholic boys in James Joyce's *A Portrait of the Artist as a Young Man*—die hard. And of course, many churches still carry Father Arnall's mantle, fulminating on hell for the unrepentant and heaven for the true believers. But Hal's case always reminds me that plenty of people who appear to live miles from Fundamentalism still worry about Heaven & Hell.

Reading Christopher Buckley's memoir, *Losing Mum and Pup,* I was astonished to realize that an intellectual giant like the author's father, William F. Buckley, harbored such simplistic notions of eternity. After scattering the ashes of his beloved friend and column syndicator Harry Elmlark, William F. turned to his son and muttered sadly, "If only he had been a Catholic."

The son writes, "Harry was a Jew and about the furthest thing from a Catholic as one could be, though come to think of it he had been happily married to one all his life. I recall being stunned by the statement. I said, 'What do you mean, Pup?' He replied matter-of-factly that as Harry was not a Catholic, he had no expectation of seeing him again in heaven.

"This hit me as a smack in the face. Pup loved Harry wholeheartedly, but rules were—apparently—rules: The gates of heaven were shut against unbelievers."[2] I was stunned not just that Buckley was so cold-heartedly certain that his lifelong friend was bound for hell, but also that he was so blithely confident of his own place in paradise *simply because he was Catholic.*

In other words, fear of losing heaven and landing in hell, and all the Manichean notions of who gets assigned where, are not merely the domain of ranting preachers and lesser minds. A lot of us are walking around with notions of eternity that are badly in need of examination.

That's why it's important at this stage to forget Heaven & Hell. The religious system only knows how to operate at the level of reward and punishment. Of course it knows of the higher strain of spiritual truth, that God's grace and mercy finally overturn all our notions of goodness and worthiness, but it can't embrace this for fear of kicking the props out from under the whole conventional, meritocratic world. The system only knows how to operate on group-think. *Only our people are going to heaven. Only our group has the Truth.* Which is why standing apart, self-differentiating, is so difficult and yet so critical. Heaven & Hell is the mainspring of conventional religion. You can't begin to escape the system as long as you're holding on to its preferred version of eternity.

But the problem is not just with the great big ugly system. It's also with you and me. When you've lived inside the fixed order for thirty or forty years, your ego has amassed remarkable power. You grow to love the reward-and-punishment system because, despite the suffering, it keeps you in control, it lets you feel superior, righteous. By criticizing yourself, lashing yourself for failing to measure up, you prove—even in your failings!—that you are really a very good person. If the prize goes to the worthy, you're still eligible.

When you abandon the whole elaborate structure of Heaven & Hell, you slip the bonds of both the conventional system and your own ego. You don't have to live in a regime that operates on false principles of performance and achievement. You can opt out.

You also don't have to live under the tyranny of your ego, fitfully trying to control everything and everybody from that inner command center. You can begin to accept what simply *is,* without needing to Photoshop reality to keep you looking good, successful, kind, and generous. You're not a "good" person; you're just a person, a man or a woman created in the image and likeness of God. All the attempts to make yourself a "good" person simply frustrate God's creation. You are already a child of God, already perfect in God's sight—despite all your obvious imperfections. The great mystery is that you are loved as is. Our great offense—our original sin, as the tradition names it—is that we reject that love. We refuse to live as the sons and daughters of God we are.

The ego can't offer that kind of love to anyone else, and it sure won't accept it from God. Only a weakling needs that kind of love, and only a loser would accept a gift offered to just anyone off the street. You're better than that, the ego insists. You'll take your chances in the world of winners and losers any day.

Every day you spend in the tit-for-tat universe of Heaven & Hell is one more day in—well, hell. That's why, for now, it has to go.

⌒

The second reason for dropping that old concept of eternity into the black plastic bag has nothing to do with the utterly false notion of who goes where and why. Instead, it's about integrating into our spirituality a realistic understanding, from contemporary physics, of time and space. It's how we separate from a credo mired in both the past and the future. Real spirituality comes to understand that everything happens *now*. As long as you are focused on some *after*life, you are blind to life in the here and now.

It's not enough to adopt a more liberal or inclusive view of eternity. Plenty of people have given up completely on the notion of hell. A recent Gallup poll found that 81 percent of Americans believe in heaven and 77 percent of those folks who believe in heaven also believe they have an "excellent" or "good" chance of going there.[3]

We solve the nasty problem of Heaven & Hell simply by going *poof,* and hell is gone. God takes everybody to heaven—and not to some literal place with gates of pearl and streets of gold. In fact, it isn't a place at all. (We're too "sophisticated" to believe that.) It's a state of union with God.

That's good, as far as it goes. But it's still the *after*life. It still happens when you die, and it's forever. This "eternity" is simply time that keeps on going and going and going. We sing,

> When we've been there ten thousand years
> Bright shining as the sun,
> We've no less days to sing God's praise,
> Than when we'd first begun.[4]

I love that old hymn, but its depiction of eternity, though poetic, is not helpful. The simple fact is, there is no time "after" death. Concepts like "before" and "after" belong to the ephemeral world of time and space. When our mortal life ends, we are freed from the limits of finitude; we enter an infinite state. That is, we join God and exist in the divine state where time and space are no more. With God, everything happens in the eternal *now*.

In Scripture, liturgy, and hymns, religion has always celebrated an eternal realm pulsing beneath the evanescent surface of this world. But I am fascinated by the way Einstein's Special Theory of Relativity illumines these spiritual realities with startling scientific clarity.

For thousands of years human beings—even the best scientific minds—were convinced that time and space were absolute. That is, an inch is an inch no matter who or where you are in the universe, as long as you have a decent ruler. And by the same token, a second is always and everywhere a second, assuming an accurate clock. But those scientific verities were shattered when Einstein demonstrated that, as a person speeds up, her perception of an inch shrinks or her perception of a second contracts. And in awesome symmetry, Einstein discovered, the mass and energy of that speeding person is expanding in exactly the reverse of the shrinking time and space factor. That is, as the speeding person approaches the velocity of light, his perceptions of time and space shrink to zero, even as his own mass and energy are expanding to infinity. In other words, at the speed of light, space dissolves and time is no more, while (if it were possible to reach light speed) the observer becomes infinite. Turns out space and time aren't absolute after all. They're *relative*.[5]

Physicists must always insert that caveat, "if it were possible to reach the speed of light," because no material thing—no spaceship or human being—can approach that speed without getting larger and larger, heavier and heavier. You would have to *be* light to dance at the speed of light. But if you could dance at that tempo, you would become infinite. That gives powerful new meaning, scientific corroboration, to the ancient words of the Bible: "God is light."

Why do I rehearse the most rudimentary Einsteinian physics? Because when we speak about *eternity* in religious discussions, people get squirrelly. Eternity is simply time that goes on forever. It goes on and on, as we pray, in *saecula saeculorum,* "world without end." Like the old major league pitcher who was asked about his future and replied, "The future is just like the present, only longer." This is the woolly thinking that underpins our basic notion of the afterlife. In this life, time is fleeting, stealing away, working against us. But in the "life to come," time will go on endlessly. It's a simple-minded wish that all the joys and pleasures of this life will be enjoyed forever in the next—"[this] world without end."

"There are cigars in Heaven," C. S. Lewis writes in *A Grief Observed.* "For that is what we should all like. The happy past restored."[6] Quantum physics sweeps all that away. It proves, scientifically, that at the light speed of eternity, space dissolves and time is no more. *There is no more time.* That is why I opened this chapter with Einstein's

words, "For those of us who believe in physics, this separation between past, present, and future is only an illusion, however tenacious."[7] If the folks who believe in physics understand the eternal now,
it's time for the people who believe in God to get the memo.

Unfortunately, however, our thinking has been so ingrained we
can hardly avoid projecting heaven and hell into some endless futurity.
Once we apply our faulty thinking to the words of the Bible, we are
set for disastrous misunderstandings. What makes it insidious is, *we
think we know!* It's patently obvious. When I studied French, the
teacher warned us about *faux amis.* They're dangerous because they
look just like English words, and you're sure you know exactly what
they mean. You read *la chair* and think it's obviously the thing you sit
on, when actually it means "the flesh."

When the Bible speaks of "finding eternal life," "entering the
kingdom of heaven" or "the kingdom of God," we think we know
exactly what these words mean, and it's always some future state.
When Jesus says, "Everyone who looks to the Son and believes in him
shall have eternal life,"[8] our ears have been trained to hear an assur-
ance that the believer is "going to heaven." Not even close. "Eternal
life" in Greek is *aionios,* literally the "ages of ages," or we might say, the
"life of the ages." While Jesus certainly foresaw a moment beyond
time when our mortal joys—at best only partial—will find ultimate
fulfillment, the "life of the ages" was on offer right here, right now.
And when people tried to postpone or reschedule this life, Jesus was
not even polite.

> Jesus said to another, "Follow me."
>
> He said, "Certainly, but first excuse me for a couple of
> days, please. I have to make arrangements for my father's
> funeral."
>
> Jesus refused. "First things first. Your business is life, not
> death. And life is urgent: Announce God's kingdom!"

Then another said, "I'm ready to follow you, Master, but first excuse me while I get things straightened out at home."

Jesus said, "No procrastination. No backward looks. You can't put God's kingdom off till tomorrow. Seize the day."[9]

Jesus was fierce about this present moment. The kingdom was now, and only now.

It makes sense, really, that we should so happily misunderstand these words. Their real meaning upends the nice, settled life we want to live inside the white picket fence. For Jesus, the kingdom was like a bolt of lightning that startles us, in the white phosphorescent light of which we see the world with stunning clarity—but only for an instant. He says,

> The kingdom of heaven is like treasure hidden in a field,
> which someone found and hid; then in his joy he goes and
> sells all that he has and buys that field.[10]

This "kingdom of heaven" is no picture of the sweet by-and-by. It is a single, arresting image of a man discovering something so precious he will shed everything to have it—now!

> Again, the kingdom of heaven is like a merchant in search of
> fine pearls; on finding one pearl of great value, he went and
> sold all that he had and bought it.[11]

These are people gone mad for beauty, for glory. They live with an urgency that frightens staid people, because they have lost all sense of time. They don't care about the past. They don't care about the future anymore. They seek one thing, and they will have it now.

Parables like this are why Annie Dillard suggested that instead of wearing straw hats and velvet bonnets to church, "we should all be wearing crash helmets."[12] To avoid something so unseemly, we took the "kingdom of heaven," which Jesus so clearly meant as an altered state of consciousness—a radically new way of seeing and reading reality—and turned it into the spiritual equivalent of a trip to Disneyland.

This is the moment to be done with sentimental and cockamamie notions of eternity, not primarily because they cloud your understanding of some "life after death," but because they rob you of your share in eternal life—now.

I want to close with those parenthetical words from the chapter title, "For Now." Rejecting the old doctrine of Heaven & Hell doesn't mean there's no such thing as a state of union with God and a state of separation from God. It doesn't mean there's nothing after you die. It doesn't mean that heaven and hell are merely what we make of this life. Affirming that eternity is happening now doesn't mean there is nothing greater in store. There is. St. Paul affirms this so memorably in 1 Corinthians 13:12, "For now we see in a mirror, dimly, but then we will see face to face. Now I know only in part; then I will know fully, even as I have been fully known." It simply means that eternity begins now. Even if we can only see it "in a mirror, dimly," we can see it!

It means that we try at least to live in what we know to be the truth. If God exists in the eternal now, then the blessed task of being human is to meet God there, in the only place where God can be found. The past does not exist. There is no future. These are just prison-house terms for the dead zones on either side of life/now. The next twelve chapters of this book are all about some aspect of living in the now. But you can't even begin to live in that place until you bid an unceremonious good-bye to Heaven & Hell.

One day you will know hell for real, the way Albert Camus knew it: "I shall tell you a great secret, my friend. Don't wait for the last judgment. It happens every day."[13] The way Franz Kafka knew it: "Only our concept of time makes it possible for us to speak of the Day of Judgment by that name; in reality it is a summary court in perpetual session."[14] One day you will know heaven for real, the way St. Teresa of Avila knew it: "All the way to heaven is heaven," (and all the way to hell is hell.)[15]

But that comes later. For now, Heaven & Hell can only cause you trouble and lead you to spiritual regression. Forget them and stand apart—at least for now.

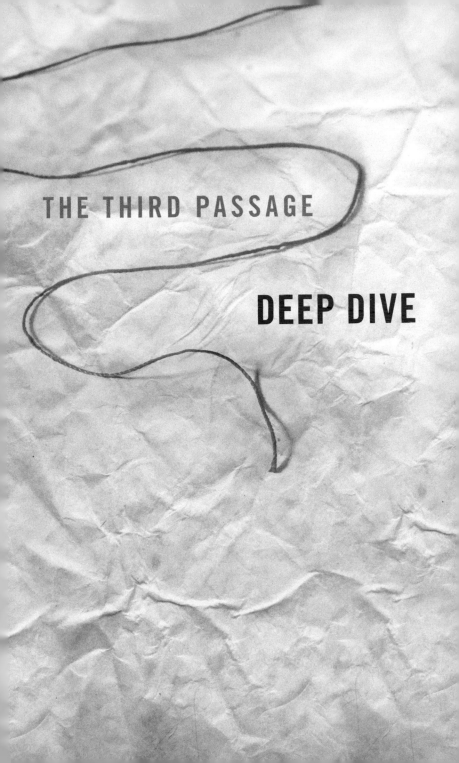

THE THIRD PASSAGE

DEEP DIVE

NINE

Heart Monitor

> All mankind's troubles are caused by one single thing,
> which is their inability to sit quietly in a room.
>
> —Blaise Pascal

For centuries, spiritual seekers have underlined one verse in the Bible and written "Aha!" in the margin. It is Matthew 6:6: "But whenever you pray, go into your room and shut the door and pray to your Father who is in secret; and your Father who sees in secret will reward you." Finally, Spiritual Life 101. The key to spirituality, Jesus says, happens when you shut the door.

Engaging your inner life always means closing out the thousand distractions, the pressing issues that demand your attention, the people who lay claim to your time and energy, the voices that presume to tell you who you are and what you must do. In his wisdom, Jesus understands the necessity of drawing the line, setting the boundary, shutting the door.

That's exactly what we've been doing in the first two passages: shutting doors. Closing the Good-Bye Gate. Standing Apart. It takes a lot of energy to establish boundaries and tend them well. It takes a lot of work to push back on old beliefs within entrenched systems, to separate yourself and stand alone. Yet the purpose of all that detachment is to free us for a deeper attachment—to God. The reason for shutting the exterior door, in Jesus's terms, is to open another, inner door. As St. Augustine wrote, "How can you draw close to God, if you are far from yourself?"[1]

This interior work is done, Jesus says, in "secret." Away from the crowds, the frenzy, the Babel. That is where we are now: ready to turn inward. It is the next passage, the Deep Dive, that will bring us into the solitary depths of our being.

That sounds like a lovely notion, but if you're like most people, you will struggle to make this next movement. You live in a noisy world, and it keeps getting noisier. All the hubbub, all the busyness is how you avoid your self. When you've lived for years in a largely externalized universe, overwhelmed with crazy busyness and hyperstress, it's not easy to decide suddenly you're going to be all Zen. In fact, once we have closed that exterior door, most of us need a little help opening the one that leads to the soul.

Yet we have to make this movement. Otherwise none of the gifts hidden along the next few passages will be available.

Ready?

<hr />

One Christmas a few years ago I received the gift of a heart monitor. I had been running for years without a cardiac thought, until the doctor asked at my checkup about my exercise regimen. I had just run my first half marathon, a race that pushed my body to its limits. I might want to check my heart rate, the doctor suggested. Mark how high it goes and how long it takes to return to normal. At lunch one day I mentioned it to a fellow runner who told me about a great monitor he used. I intended to get one but I forgot about it, until I opened his gift.

The day after Christmas I strapped the sensor to my chest and the monitor to my wrist. I was going to give it a run.

As it received the first impulses from the sensor, the heart icon on the wrist monitor pulsed. I walked a block and watched the numbers creep up. I broke into a jog, and my heart revved in response. I increased speed to my normal running pace, and the rate crept up, leveled off and held its place. After a mile I stopped. Walking, I stared at my wrist as the readout blinked lower and lower.

The rest of that three-mile run was like driving a car. It was as if my body had a tachometer. I knew exactly what my ticker was doing. When I climbed a slight hill, I checked my wrist. I couldn't *feel* my heart pumping any faster, but the LED didn't lie. This incline was exacting two beats more per minute.

The ease with which I could monitor every changing beat of my heart made me curious. What if we could sink a probe deep down into our heart of hearts? What if we could monitor *that* heart?

In the ascendant years of youth and early adulthood we spend most of our time attending to the outer shell of our lives. That's pretty easy to monitor; the world tells you how you're doing. You get loud-and-clear messages that tell you if you're looking good, making the right friends, hitting the right parties. You don't have to ask if you're successful, or if your children are included in the preferred playgroups. The system has subtle and blatant ways of notifying you. You always know your status, how you're doing.

In that world, though, it's hard to get a read on your soul. After a while most of us are sick and tired of living in a place where what counts is on the surface. Unless you're Donald Trump, there inevitably comes a point when we're done with all the gewgaws of the good life. A powerful urge overtakes us and we have to know if there's anything solid and everlasting *in here,* or whether we are, in T. S. Eliot's terms, "hollow men."[2]

The Irish poet Patrick Kavanagh sings of this urge in "Pegasus." He begins,

My soul was an old horse
Offered for sale in twenty fairs.

He sells his soul-horse to the church, but "the buyers were little men who feared his unusual airs." Then he sells to the "men of State," who wonder if another body would better fit his tail. After a week of labor "he came back a hurdle of bones, / Starved, overworked, in despair." He feeds him roadside grass, nurses him to health—to peddle him once again. "I lowered my price." Now the creature is offered for the meanest work. "He'll draw your dungiest cart." But no one will take the worn-out, spavined horse. Not one bid. Finally his despair turns to revelation.

"Soul," I prayed,
"I have hawked you through the world
Of Church and State and meanest trade.
But this evening, halter off,
Never again will it go on.
On the south side of ditches
There is grazing of the sun.
No more haggling with the world...."
As I said these words he grew
Wings upon his back. Now I may ride him
Every land my imagination knew.[3]

After you have pimped your soul to every crass and brutal buyer out there, you end up with nothing. Now you have to look within and see who you really are.

That inner space, however, is terra incognita. We do not know our own souls.

Years ago, after Sputnik and the launch of *Star Trek,* America was agog over space travel. We used all our national might to send rockets and probes millions of miles into space. Meanwhile, right here on earth, oceanographers noted rucfully that we were completely ignorant of the dazzling world that lay not two hundred feet below the surface of the ocean.

That upward, outward thrust is typical of early-stage development, for nations as well as for individuals. We're totally fascinated by what's *out there,* utterly heedless of what lies *in here. Semper sursum* is the motto of countless schools and colleges. "Always upward!" Aiming high, always rising. That's the early trajectory of life. It's no wonder we're clueless when, like Icarus, we fall from the sky. Now we must go deep inside. But how? What skills or experience is necessary? If we need a guide for this endeavor, where would we find one?

It's no shame to need a little guidance. Dante needed Virgil for his descent into purgatory and hell. Virgil I'm not, but I can show you the ladder that goes down.

Yes, every true spiritual quest leads you first *down.*

Dante drops down. Odysseus descends into the underworld, only there meeting the prophet Tiresias who shows him how to get home to Ithaca. Plato's prisoners are trapped in a cave before they can ascend to freedom. Faust goes down. Melville's Captain Ahab must search the ocean depths. Jonah is three days in the belly of the whale; and just so, says the Bible, Christ is three days and three nights in the belly of the earth. I once Googled "Twelve Steps," expecting to find just the list. Instead I landed on a site that depicted a staircase with twelve steps. Down. They go *down!*

There is no great ascent without first a descent. Yet all popular religions give you a staircase that goes *up.* That's what you need for the first leg of life's journey. In the end it's the wrong direction. But the baffling mystery is that you must make the wrong moves first. You can't get it right the first time. You must imagine that you will be the first human to climb the ladder of success…and just keep climbing. You must be overtaken with hubris.

Near the end of his life, Carl Jung could say, "In my case Pilgrim's Progress consisted in my having to climb down a thousand ladders until I could reach out my hand to the little clod of earth that I am."[4]

It's as old as the Garden of Eden, the Fall. People still madly in the *semper-sursum* phase of life are deathly afraid of the fall. But by the time you've gotten a few years under your belt, you know better. It's not just lonely at the top, it's shallow, cold, and meaningless. You fall (or more likely, get pushed), and you find out it's okay down here. After that long flirtation with the heights, you're ready to stop fighting the fall.

When I was a child, I liked to paddle to the deep end of the swimming pool, then, slowly exhaling, let myself drift to the bottom. There I would sit cross-legged on what felt like the ocean floor. For a pale-blue minute I sat in a solitary world. I could hear nothing except a heartbeat thudding my eardrum; the splash and laughter above sounded like muffled noise from a parallel world. Here I was alone, totally aware of my being. Later in life when I learned to scuba dive, I had an even more profound sense of being alone in a world far from the madding crowd, a world so quiet I could hear only the rush of oxygen on my in-breath and the rumble of bubbles carrying my out-breath to the surface. To hear my every breath was calming yet enlivening, like a baby sleeping on my shoulder, a cat purring in my lap.

If you've had this kind of experience yourself, it will come as no surprise that the practice of prayer from East to West in every tradition begins with the simplest act: breathe in, breathe out.

Try it. Sit still, close your eyes, and notice your inhale and your exhale. If you do it for a few minutes, you will find yourself drifting down to the bottom of that ocean. You will come into a deeper awareness of your self.

You don't have to be a mystic or a monk to do this. After all, every hospital in the country now offers breathing exercises just like this to patients who are struggling with pain, illness, and their attendant anxiety. They do it in hospitals because it *works*. It brings you into possession of your own self so that anxiety and pain cannot take over your whole being. *You* are greater than your anxiety, than your pain, and in that state you can find peace even if the pain never goes away. Somehow it's all right. But you don't have to wait until a trauma breaks to learn in some hospital how to make contact with your own self. In fact, it's much better to go ahead and start now.

So I'm going to ask you to be still. You don't have to assume the lotus position or get on your knees. You do have to be quiet, though. And alone.

What you're after is not any*thing*. It's simply an awareness. You know the three keys to real estate: location, location, location. Here are the three keys to spirituality: awareness, awareness, awareness. When you cultivate simple awareness, you begin to see not into an obscure spiritual realm, but into the plain reality before you. (More on this in chapter 12.) It's like waking from a sleepwalk. You showed up in all those places—work, home, restaurants, parties—but you have no recollection of anything. Now you notice what was there all along. But you can't do that amid all the noise and busyness. You must quiet down, and then it just happens. It happens *to you*. The act of stilling yourself is important but only provisional. Then you must watch and wait.

This might be harder than it sounds. If you have experienced any of what the world calls success, you know how to get what you need. You go for it. Make it happen. Seize the payday. Sometimes grabbing the initiative works, so we imagine that it works for everything. Not so. This is soul work, and the soul has its own ways.

Parker Palmer writes,

> The soul is a wild animal—tough resilient, savvy, and self-sufficient.... Yet despite its toughness, the soul is also shy. Just like a wild animal, it seeks safety in the dense underbrush, especially when other people are around. If we want to see a wild animal, the last thing we should do is go crashing through the woods, shouting for the creature to come out. But if we are willing to walk quietly into the woods and sit patiently at the base of a tree, breathe with the earth, and fade into our surroundings, the wild creature we seek may put in an appearance. We may see it briefly and only out of the corner of an eye—but the sight is a gift we will always treasure as an end in itself.[5]

I knew a man in Illinois who did just this. Doug lived on the edge of town where there were still tracts of open prairie, land he had worked to preserve from development. Before the sun came up, he would walk into the high Big Bluestem (a million-year-old prairie grass he said was almost extinct) and sit down. He'd wait there for an hour, silently. And then, he told me, out of the half light would come deer, pheasant, rabbits, birds. They'd nearly brush his leg walking by.

This was years ago. I loved Doug, but I thought he was a little nutty. I know now why I thought so. I was in my *semper-sursum* years. I didn't get it.

I'm still not the kind of person who sits in the woods. But that's not the point. We're not all supposed to become Thoreau. The point is, you have to unlearn your old, clutchy ways and let go a little. Quiet down. The second act of your life is about to open. The theater sounds a chime, and the house lights dim. That's your clue to take your seat, turn off your cell phone, stop talking to your friends. All you have to do now is sit and see. The curtain will go up, and your life story will be enacted. It *will* happen! Your only job is to pay attention to your own life.

Look around you: half the people haven't even come back from the bathroom yet. They're still at the bar, having a cigarette out the back door. The other half is standing in the aisles talking and texting. It's as if they can't hear the chime, don't catch the dimming lights. You wonder, *How could they not notice all the signals? How could they miss their own lives?* It probably feels funny sitting down when no one else seems to be. But this is an act of self-differentiation. It will always feel like nobody else is doing this, that you're the only one, that everybody is enjoying a perfectly fine life without sitting down, without being quiet, without paying attention. Be quiet anyway. Good things are about to happen.

I am not so concerned that you learn how to pray or meditate right now. The next two passages will take you there. I want you simply to have a regular experience of quiet and aloneness to open your awareness to the spiritual world resting just below the frothy surface of life. You can take a walk. You can work in your garden or in your woodshop. You can paint or draw or journal or make music. Some people practice yoga.

I knew an older priest who lived in a retirement center. Many priests pray the Divine Office daily in a chapel or in a corner of their bedroom. But Al told me that at his age he had the words and Psalms of Morning Prayer by heart, so he prayed in the lap pool. Back and forth. On the in-breath it was *O Lord open thou my lips,* and on the out-breath, *And my mouth shall show forth thy praise.* Breathe in, *Create in me a pure heart, O God;* breathe out, *And renew a right spirit within me.*

It doesn't matter where or how you do it (and here personality type plays a big role in spiritual development), but you must find time to be alone, still, aware.

The twelfth-century Christian mystic Hugh of St. Victor believed that human beings were endowed with three sets of eyes: the eye of flesh, the eye of reason, and the eye of contemplation. This latter is the third eye, by which the soul sees not only within itself but also above itself to God.[6]

Every spiritual tradition understands that humans are essentially blind to the world of spirit. We need some other, inner eye to espy the realm of formless unity underlying this raucous and fractious world of forms, to sense the energy that binds everything together, the essence that gives it all meaning and purpose—glory, even. This you cannot see unless you open the eye of the heart.

When you get quiet and open your eyes (as I used to do sitting on the bottom of the pool), things just appear. It's not that you see visions or images or anything that would count as religious or spiritual. You just see what's there. For what feels like the first time. Once you descend to this place of quiet, you get a glimpse of what's real, what matters. You know something deep and true. What you learn is a sixth-sense kind of knowledge. It's nothing you could point out to anyone else. You can hardly describe it to yourself.

This does not happen overnight; the impatient will miss it by a few days. So keep being still. All your little gremlins will crawl out and demand immediate attention, all the voices in your head will prattle on and talk over one another. But since they have no depth or capacity, they always run out of energy, like a child's wild tantrum collapsing eventually in exhaustion, and then you will be alone at the bottom of the sea.

You don't have to be good at this (that's only your ego talking); you just have to hear the chime and see the dimming lights.

Sit down.

Be quiet.

Open your third eye.

TEN

Original You

> Why are you unhappy?
> Because 99.9 percent
> Of everything you think
> And of everything you do,
> Is for yourself—
> And there isn't one.
>
> —Wei Wu Wei

> *Noverim me, noverim te!*
> "I would know myself, in order to know you!"
>
> —St. Augustine

In the opening pages of his autobiographical novel, *The Power of One*, Bryce Courtenay tells a terrifying and triumphant story. It begins with a five-year-old English boy living in South Africa in the 1930s. His father has been killed by a rogue elephant and, after a nervous breakdown, his mother has disappeared to a sanitarium. The boy is alone, raised now by his Zulu nanny who sends the boy off to a boarding school. But he is the only English-speaking boy in a Boer school where all the boys speak Afrikaans. The memory of the Boer War, the British troops who killed their fathers and grandfathers, is still fresh for these Boer boys. They hate the English, and they take it out on the newest boy (who is also the youngest by two years).

Little Peekay is the target of angry ridicule and taunting persecution. Terrified, the six-year-old begins to wet his bed at night. The other boys find out of course, and he is forced to drag his mattress out, wash it, and dry it in the sun. The gang leaders assemble a kangaroo court and put Peekay on trial. The "storm troopers" tie strips of rags over his eyes and stand him in the dock. He is convicted and sentenced to a punishment that cruelly fits the crime. He kneels in the shower while the Boer boys urinate on him. This goes on, day after day, until finally the term is over and Peekay goes home on break. There he collapses in his nanny's arms. In tears he tells her of his nightmare, and she sends for the medicine man, Inkosi-Inkosikazi, who can cure the boy of his "night water" problem.

Four days later an enormous black Buick pulls up. Slowly, out of the backseat emerges a Zulu man who seems a hundred years old, barefoot, with a mangy leopard skin cloak falling from his shoulders. He walks under the nearest tree, lays a mat on the ground, and summons the boy. Fearful, Peekay clings to his nanny, but she nudges him forward. It is an honor, she says, for the great chief may only ask another chief to sit with him on the *indaba* mat of "meeting."

"Now," says the old man with beady eyes like a rooster, "this unfortunate business of the night water." Peekay is both frightened and hopeful. From an old leather bag the shaman produces the twelve magic shinbones of the white ox. He mumbles a dark incantation and throws the bones on the ground with a clatter. Sitting on his haunches, the wise man studies the yellowed bone-dice for clues to the boy's problem.

"Close your eyes," the medicine man commands the boy, "not tight, but as if your eyes were tired, your eyelids heavy." The old man puts the boy into a trance-sleep. Peekay hears a sudden roar and sees three waterfalls. Below he sees a river with ten stones crossing it.

Inkosi-Inkosikazi says, "You are standing on a rock above the highest waterfall. A young warrior who has killed his first lion. You are wearing the skirt of lion tail as you face the setting sun. Now the sun has passed beyond Zululand. You can see the moon rising over Africa and you are at peace with the night.

"You must take a deep breath and say the number three to yourself as you leap. Then, when you surface, you must take another breath and say the number two as you are washed across the rim of the second waterfall, then again a deep breath and you rise and are carried over the third. Now you must swim to the first stone, counting backward from ten to one, counting each stone as you leap from it to the next to cross the rushing river."

The old man pauses. "You must jump now, little warrior of the king!" And in his reverie the boy dives. He plunges into the night, into the deep pool, surfaces, is swept *three-two-one* across the waterfalls. Then he swims to the first stone glistening in the moonlight. Jumping *ten, nine, eight, seven, six, five, four, three, two, one* he crosses the rushing river, then falls exhausted on the white sandy beach.

The river roars beside him and the waters roar within him, but through it comes Inkosi-Inkosikazi's voice. "We have crossed the night water to the other side and it is done. You must open your eyes, little warrior." There is nothing more to fear. Peekay awakes from his dream-vision, and the medicine man says, "When you need me you may come to the night country. I will always be there in the place of the three waterfalls and the ten stones across the river."

The story continues, told now in the voice of the man Peekay grew to become. He returns to school. He never wet his bed again, but that did not stop the bullies. They were Boers, after all. He was English. They dragged him out at night, but their power over him was broken.[1]

"Down there in the night country, by the waterfalls, I was safe from the storm troopers. As they tied the dirty piece of rag over my eyes, I would take three deep breaths. Immediately I would hear Inkosi-Inkosikazi's voice, soft as distant thunder. 'You are standing on the rock above the highest waterfall, a young warrior who has killed his first lion....' I stood in the moonlight on the rock above the three waterfalls.... Far below I could see the ten stones glistening and the white water as it crashed through the narrow gorge beyond. I knew then that the person on the outside was only a shell, a presence to be provoked. Inside was the real me, where my tears joined the tears of all the sad people in the whole world to form the three waterfalls in the night country."[2]

Here is a boy who discovers within him an *I* that cannot be touched by bullies, a self that is not fazed by any exterior violence, an *I* that is at peace with the night, a being that finds its strength and power by diving down, down, down.

In the early phase of faith, you totter precariously on the pinnacle. You are nervous with the night. You cling to all the external markers of success, and you desperately need other people to tell you you're okay. So you are vulnerable to the vagaries of others' esteem. If the important people think you're cool and happening and wonderful, you're all right. But the in crowd always turns on you, and then you are crushed. They take you out, tie dirty rags over your eyes, and abuse you. All you can do is cower, go home, and cry in Nanny's bosom. Now is the time to sit down with the man in the huge black Buick.

I told you that this section of the trail is a watershed, that unless you find a way to go deep within, none of the gifts hidden within the following passages will be available to you—because there is no *you* to take delivery. It's time to find the unassailable self that lies beneath the *you* that has been built up, defended, and shown to the world, "offered for sale," like Patrick Kavanagh's soul-horse, "in twenty fairs."

When you locate this self and take the first tentative steps of living inside this hidden *you,* it is quite literally like being a new person in a different world. The things that used to frighten you don't so much anymore. The things that used to motivate you seem pointless. That's because your whole orientation is shifting from *out there* to *in here.* Once you start living inside this inner *I,* spiritual truths that used to clang off the back rim of your heart become slam dunks. All the frightful paradoxes—losing your life to find it, going down the up staircase, glorying (with St. Paul) in your weakness—make a new kind of sense. You're ready for the next, deeper level of spiritual formation. But only when you have settled into that deep, inner self.

This is *so* beyond self-esteem! That is what we lovingly offer to children and young people. We help them to accommodate themselves to the demands of the world so that they can be accepted and valued at the "twenty fairs." But after you have played that game for thirty or forty years, and have been peed on by the people whose acceptance and affirmation you craved, you say, "No more!"

As Hermann Hesse puts it, "A man who is 'ill-adjusted' to the world is always on the verge of finding himself. One who is adjusted to the world never finds himself, but gets to be a cabinet minister."[3] All right? You're done with the world's self-esteem. You want, in fact, a real self.

This self is not something you create, like that earlier ego-made self. It is something you catch a glimpse of, feel rising within. It is, in fact, your original self. It was there from your birth, has been there all along. It's just that the system demanded another version of you, and you did what we all do: you gave it to them. They believed in that confected person, and after a while you believed your own performance. You forgot about that original *I.* From time to time it tried to assert itself: in the moment when you wanted to take piano but all your friends were going out for football so you did too, or the time you felt like wearing your hair curly and red and blowzy but all your friends were dyeing their hair blond and ironing it straight so you did too.

You successfully quashed that other *I;* you had to in those days, and it almost went away for good and stopped embarrassing you. But later in life, usually when the front-and-center *you* has tottered and fallen one too many times, that original self makes one more bold attempt to surface. *Now?* it seems to say. *Will you have me now?*

Thomas Merton called that front-and-center *you* the "false self," and that hidden, original *you* he called the "true self."[4]

For Thomas Keating, the Trappist monk who fathered the Centering Prayer movement, the front-and-center *you* is the fragile self, wounded in childhood and exiled in adolescence.[5] It is defined by all the coping mechanisms we have developed to protect those wounds, numb all that pain.

The whole enterprise of the first half of life is the building of that false self, and since it always eventually collapses, the gift of the midlife crisis is that it can dethrone the pretender self and welcome the ascent of the royal self that has been moldering in the soul's dark dungeon all these years.

Remember, the false self is, by definition, created by you, but the true self simply *is.* If allowed, it will simply appear. It does not need you to help it, any more than a butterfly needs you to help it emerge from its cocoon. All it needs is for you to stop squashing it whenever it tries to emerge. It takes a reverse kind of work to simply let it be.

If I could explain to you how it takes so much work to learn how to do nothing, I would. But I don't even understand it myself. All I know is that the paradox works. At this level, where the wild and beautiful stuff starts happening, the key skill for all of us can-do people is non-action.

I stress this because your first instinct will be to go after your true self with the same tactics that helped you to successfully build the false one. You will go to retreats and spiritual workshops looking for *the* answer, seeking enlightenment like one more commodity you are so good at snagging. You may even change your hairstyle, grow a goatee, wear some new habit that looks vaguely monastic, ditch the Beemer and drive a hybrid instead. The ego has endless ways of changing the window dressing and staying in power. This quest is different. You have to die.

Now I am going to tell you a little more than I know.

This dying is a tricky business. The only clue I have to offer lies in the three keys to spirituality. Whenever I am stumped, I come back to them: awareness, awareness, awareness.

This dying is nothing you *do*. After all, your ego will always kill the wrong thing: your own petty sins and obsessions, or other evil people who are obviously the cause of all your suffering. If the right self—the false one—is to die, it will happen, ironically enough, when you do nothing.

That may sound like a cheap koan, but unroll your eyes and stay with me.

Until you realize how much energy you pour into the creation, maintenance, repair, and redecorating of that false self (and you can't see that without those three keys), you will never understand how just doing nothing is so beautifully right.

Because the false self is not real—it's a fake, made-up thing—you have to work endlessly to keep it going. Traditional spiritual language says it must die, and it will. You don't have to kill it. The fact is, it has a life expectancy of only about thirty or forty years. Once its program of success and achievement (including your personal exemption from the normal aging process) hits the wall, it's hospice time. Now you must simply stop propping it up; let it pass away. But the false self never goes quietly. It tends to shake off its rigor mortis and come back for another appearance. (This is always more obvious in others than in ourselves.)

But eventually death comes for the old self. It is not something you do, so much as something you allow. It comes, you nod.

St. Paul, who spoke of a new man and an old man struggling within him, cried out, "Who will rescue me from this body of death?"[6] Paul was baffled: the more fiercely he fought against the old man of death, the more closely clung that old corpse. It's like a Chinese finger trap: the harder you pull, the tighter your bondage. Finally Paul understood that only Someone else could free him. Paul's job was to trust and do nothing. And what does it take to do that? Right. Those three keys.

We are naturally afraid to let the old self die, because it has succeeded in convincing us that it's the only self we've got. It's easier to allow this dying if you can glimpse within you another, hidden being who is set to emerge—once the false self is gone.

It took me a long while before I could recognize this self-in-waiting. For years I heard those words of Jesus: "Whoever wants to be my disciple must deny themselves and take up their cross daily and follow me. For whoever wants to save their life will lose it, but whoever loses their life for me will save it."[7]

Deny yourself, and lose your life. I preached on those words. But I was in over my head. I knew mostly what it wasn't—self-abasement, self-flagellation, demeaning myself in the name of religion. I knew that wasn't it. I just couldn't put my finger on what had to be denied and lost. I couldn't figure out how to die and so to live. And I sure couldn't tell anyone else how to do that.

My problem was simple. I was trying to penetrate second-half-of-life wisdom with a first-half mind.

I will always remember when the light clicked on. I was listening to Anthony de Mello, an Indian Jesuit who wove together the spirituality of East and West. In his inimitable way, Tony de Mello revealed the deep, original *I* beneath the *me* I present to the world.[8] No one had ever shown me that before. I was gobsmacked. *That* is the true self that longs to live in and through me. I could not possess it because it is actually the still point where my life and the life of God coincide. All I could do was welcome it, reverence it.

Once I sensed the presence of that awesome *I,* I also knew its shadow, the ersatz version I had been taught to dress up and clop through the world like a Ken doll. *That* is the self that needed to die. It made all the sense in the world! Now when Jesus said, "Deny yourself," I knew exactly who he meant. And because it freed that other *I* within me—if only for a luminous moment—that kind of dying and denying was not grim sacrifice but pure joy.

This is red-hot powerful stuff. But be careful. If you haven't begun to unhook from conventional notions of life in the System, if Toto hasn't pulled back the curtain on the old Wizard "God," if you haven't even glimpsed your own ego—much less challenged its dominance—you have no way of understanding this crucial dying. If you do not understand which self must be denied, what life you must lose, you can do yourself and others a lot of damage. Your ego can kill off a lot of other things in order to save itself.

We see the ego's influence in conventional faith. Every religion insists that something must die so that a new life can emerge. But little-mind religion has always marked the wrong thing for death. Fearful, egoic religion always points *out there*! The stranger, the enemy, the one-not-like-us must be killed. We have to burn the witches, the heretics, the traitors. We have to excommunicate, ban, exile, shun, condemn. It's the women who threaten us, or the gays or the people of color. It's the Jews or the Muslims or the immigrants.

The unchecked ego has an enemy list that makes Richard Nixon look calm and secure. All so that you never have to look inside and find, like Pogo, that the enemy is within.

Or religion might tell you that the self is the body. That's what has to die. So we have centuries of mortification. Hair shirts, thumb-screws, self-flagellation, cold showers, piercings, sleeping on boards.

Or the demon is food or sex or alcohol or some other fearful pleasure.

The hard truth is that the self which conventional religion marks for death is often, tragically, your original self, the one seeking freedom and the full expression of its power and beauty. It is the self that threatens the enforcers of the norm. "What must die," they say, "is whatever draws you from the one true expression of life as we define it." Here again, all the "misfits" of our world—the artists, the blind seers, the poor, the obvious sinners, and those who haunt the margins—are a constant threat to the order of the System.

Winston Churchill put it this way:

> The world naturally looks with some awe upon a person who appears unconcernedly indifferent to home, money, comfort, rank, or even power and fame. The world feels not without a certain apprehension that here is someone outside its jurisdiction; someone before whom its allurements may be spread in vain; someone strangely enfranchised, untamed, untrammelled by convention, moving independently of the ordinary currents of human action.[9]

So, living in a world that demands the sham self and rewards its triumphs, living in a religious culture that consistently gets it wrong, how do we let the false self die and the true self live? As I said a moment ago, the true self (like the cocooned butterfly) does not need your help to emerge. It will happen *unless you stop it.*

Jungian psychologist James Hollis dramatically underscores this truth. The true self (Jung's term for which is simply *Self* with a capital *S*) is not some milquetoast character, he assures us, who will sit quietly by. It is, in fact, an underground operative, working to overthrow the false self:

> A mystery so profound that none of us really seems to grasp it until it has indisputably grasped us, is that some force transcendent to ordinary consciousness is at work within us to bring about our ego's overthrow. No, it is not some malevolent demon, though we often project our search for such a slippery spirit on our partner or our employer or even our children. That force, paradoxically, is the *Self,* the architect of wholeness, which operates from a perspective larger than conventional consciousness. How could the ego ever come to understand, let alone accept, that its overthrow is engineered from within?[10]

Hollis depicts a struggle for ascendancy within every human soul. The small-*s* self is mostly in power, running the ego show for the first thirty or forty years. Then its program begins to wear out and fail. It can't deliver on its promises, so you begin to interrogate the false self (that's what you're doing when you're talking to yourself at 3:00 a.m. in a state of anxiety or ugly depression). That's the moment when the Self attempts to get your attention. *There's another way of living,* it whispers, *another way of seeing the world, another way of counting success. Quite literally, another way of seeing your Self.*

The inner turmoil we experience when we're in crisis, depression, or some other dark valley, Hollis says, is actually the Self pushing up against the self, pressing to come out of its darkness and into the light.[11] We may feel a malevolent force is oppressing us, but what is happening is in fact a Jacob-and-Esau struggle in our depths. Which one will be firstborn? Which one will become the dominant expression of our life?

Good news: the pain and the suffering of the true self overcoming the false self are birth pangs. More good news: you don't have to go find some new you; it is already there within. Now it senses an opportunity. At just the moment when your false self is falling apart, your original self urges to be born again. And it will happen. *Unless you stop it.* Unless you are so afraid of your own light and grace and power that you turn back to the sad comfort of the old false self.

So let it be born. Even though this shimmering being frightens you and you are not sure how in the world you can live within it, let it be born. Trust it. Like Peekay. Because deep within you is an *I* that cannot be touched by the "slings and arrows of outrageous fortune," cannot be moved either by exhilaration or depression because it simply *is,* does not need anything, will not grow old, cannot die.

St. Augustine, who lived like a hellion in his false self, finally glimpsed this other being within him and declared with awe, *interior intimo meo et superior summo meo.* God is "more inward than my innermost and higher than my uppermost."[12]

When you learn to quiet down and go to that deep place within, you too will be awed to discover this original self, which is *interior intimo meo et superior summo meo,* a being that is not God but that is completely bounded and penetrated by the divine.

St. Patrick's Breastplate is a Celtic masterpiece that understands so well this inner self-in-God:

Christ be with me, Christ within me
Christ behind me, Christ before me
Christ beside me, Christ to win me
Christ to comfort and restore me

Christ beneath me, Christ above me
Christ in quiet, Christ in danger
Christ in hearts of all that love me
Christ in mouth of friend and stranger.[13]

That original self is burning within you. The first feverish run for temporal glory has petered out, and this self-in-God is surging out of your depths. This is its appointed hour.

Do not hinder it.

Let it rise.

ELEVEN

Befriending the Wolf Within

> He was in the wilderness for forty days, tempted by
> Satan; and he was with the wild beasts.
>
> —Mark 1:13

I t was the week before Christmas when the phone rang. Pam answered it. I was sitting at the kitchen table reading the newspaper.

"Just a minute," she said, and I knew it was for me. When she walked into the kitchen with the phone in hand, I could tell something was a little odd. Pam shrugged as if to say, "I don't know who it is" and handed me the receiver.

"Hello," I said, and a voice came back in a whisper, "This is Rob." I could barely make out the words. This wasn't the hoarse, muted voice of someone with winter laryngitis; this was a voiceless whisper. I didn't know what to think. Rob was a friend who had moved a few years ago to Arizona. He used to join me in the chapel for Morning Prayer. Sometimes it was just the two of us, and we would pray for one another. Soon after he left, we exchanged a couple of letters, but I hadn't heard from him in months.

"How are you?" I said, figuring something was plainly wrong.

The breath came back: "I've been to the doctor, and I'm dreadfully sick." I paused for a moment, then told him how sorry I was, especially to be so far away. He told me a few ominous details of his cancer. It was all so sudden. He asked me to pray for him, and I assured him that I would.

Then I said, "How did you lose your voice?"

He whispered, "One of my vocal cords is paralyzed."

"And what," I asked, "causes such a condition?"

He paused, then squeaked out the words, "They tell me it's idiopathic."

Since I did not know the meaning of that baleful medical term, I just repeated the word, "Idiopathic?"

In a moment Rob's one good vocal cord fluttered lamely and the words leaked out, "It means self-caused." I realized that I was speaking with a man who was quite literally paralyzed by fear.

Now that we have made the deep dive within, we may speak of fear.

The System is geared only for up, can only sing, "Accentuate the positive, eliminate the negative." It has no capacity for paradox, so it cannot deal with fear. When you have braved the descent and made that first, tentative contact with your original self, however, you know that the highest gifts are accessed at the lowest level—that you can't get to love without facing your deepest fears.

That is the next passage that you and I must navigate.

Authentic spirituality will always take you down, because the divine mysteries are always hidden in the darkness. It is, as St. John of the Cross called it, a "luminous darkness,"[1] but it's dark; it feels like you need the spiritual equivalent of night-vision goggles. If you simply stay in the darkness for a time, however, you find that your eyes adjust and you can see—very well, in fact.

What you are seeing is reality. Seeing it for the first time. The happy, always-up culture tries to create a positive experience by dividing life into good/bad, happy/sad, light/dark—and stuffing all the bad/sad/dark into the cellar. It's where we bury all our worries and fears, all our failures, our shame, our secrets, our depressions and addictions. "You're better off not thinking about those things," it says. But whenever we get alone, quiet down and open the third eye (chapter 9), whenever we undergo the struggle in our depths between the dying and rising self (chapter 10), we come down into that cellar and confront our fears. The flight impulse always kicks in, but if we have the grace to stay in the cellar, we start to discover a freedom down here, a spaciousness, a rounded beauty.

It's like seeing a drawing of a lion, then seeing a lion walking, sinews rippling, right in front of you. Suddenly you're seeing light *and* shadow. You see holistically. The whole picture: good and evil, pleasure and pain, beauty and dread, life and death. It's all held together down here and it's all good, since God pronounced the whole creation "very good."

Because God can hold together a *both/and* world, you can too. The key is to hold still and to trust. If you can stay down with your fears without running, that's when midnight begins to glow.

When our daughters were six and four, they decided they wanted pierced ears. Their beautiful mother, whose bejeweled ears they envied, thought it was cute. I was against it. "Do you really want someone to take a needle and push it through your earlobe?" I asked, hoping the graphic description would put an end to their fantasy. It didn't.

The day came. I took them to the mall. First Maggy sat on the stool. The man marked the spot with a black marker. Then he picked up a jewelry-store version of a rivet gun and, with one pop, pierced her ear and left a silver stud in place.

Maggy was not only older, she was also a pell-mell kid who ran fearlessly after her young life. Sharon, on the other hand, was our brooder. She was tentative, multiphobic. When Maggy jumped down from the stool with her two pierced ears, I wondered if Sharon, having seen the rivet gun, would balk. She didn't. She sat there stoically while the man put the black dots on her unblemished earlobes. I hurt for her, as I watched her brave little face. When the gun popped, she did not flinch, but a single tear leapt from her right eye and ran down her cheek.

Sharon was clearly frightened, but she did not run. She wanted something good and beautiful, and she was willing to sit with her fear until the gift appeared. Then, of course, the fear ebbs away. Pain is still real, still there, but it takes its place now alongside—inseparable from—beauty.

Something very like that is the key here—to sit with your fear. To know it so well it becomes not an enemy but an old friend. Here is where wise men and women are formed, people with deep, spacious souls.

"He's always just put out of his mind anything that's disturbing," she said. It was her husband we were talking about. He was nearly broke, had lost almost everything when the real-estate bubble popped, and now his sister was dying. They were so close, and he was in despair.

"Does he talk to you about it, or would he talk to me?" I asked.

"No, he doesn't want to talk about his troubles," she said. "That's the way it was in his childhood home—that's how you dealt with unpleasantness. You just put it away and that was that. I've told him, 'You can't keep bottling this up inside. It's not good for you.' But that's just his way."

There is nothing unusual about this man. We all do this. It's a common coping technique *because it works.*

In the early years, when you get hit with disappointments and losses, you learn to slough them off and move on. You don't have time to be all introspective. The baby has croup, and your boss is demand-ing a report by 9:00 a.m. Winners play through pain. After you go home, turn out the lights, and fall into bed, however, the wolves start howling down in the underworld. You learn to live like that for years.

Later on, things change. Usually it's because there's one wolf we can't escape, and when we undergo the suffering (because we *have* to), we find that we are still alive, sometimes stronger! Now the poles begin shifting.

If you've put even a little distance between you and the System, if you've glimpsed even briefly the *I* that is not fazed by success or fail-ure, you've seen behind the veil—and you're not so afraid anymore. If what you fear holds no real power over you, why the silent scream? If the subject of attack is just that old false self, it's not exactly a crisis. You've already seen it for what it is. It's Peekay's outer shell. Inside is the authentic you, and that cannot be touched. When you begin to understand your fears in this way, you are on the threshold of enor-mous power.

There are only two poles in life: fear and love. Each pole operates on a completely different energy source. Fear fuels the false, egoic self. Love infuses the true. One is fission, the other fusion. That is, fear in its *fission* must divide the world into those dualisms: good/ bad, happy/sad, light/dark. It tries to keep you up in the light, look-ing good, and it sends all the dark things down to the cellar. Love, on the other hand, in its *fusion* is always holding the opposites together. Yin and yang. That is the source of its creativity and beauty.

When all your personal energy goes into protecting the sham self, fear abounds. The ego sees a threat behind every bush, so panic is continual. Its fissile strategy is to deny, cut off, circle the wagons, re-fuse admittance, protect the asset at all costs.

When you know you have another *I* that doesn't need to be pro-tected, love abounds. It's not afraid of the truth—what simply *is*. It doesn't need to defend itself, doesn't need to hide its darkness, its weakness, its wounds. Love's strategy is to embrace all. When you trust the transcendent power of love, you can do the unthinkable: lift the portcullis, open the iron gate, drop the drawbridge over the moat, and let the enemies in. Like that old saying, "Fear knocked on the door. Love answered. There was no one there."

This is powerful, transformative work, but surrendering yourself to love is about the hardest thing you can do. We are all like the mouse in that ancient Indian fable. The poor creature was in constant distress because of its fear of the cat. A magician took pity on it and turned it into a cat. But then it became afraid of the dog. So the magician turned it into a panther, whereupon it was full of fear of the hunter. At this point the magician gave up. He turned it into a mouse again, saying, "Nothing I do for you is going to be of any help because you have the heart of a mouse."

You need a change of heart (I know because I have a mouse heart myself). It seems crazy to welcome our fears, to open the cellar door, and walk down those steps. And it *is* crazy…in life's early stages. Now, however, it starts to make its own kind of sense.

For many years when I lived near Philadelphia, I enjoyed listening to a public radio program called *Voices in the Family,* with Dr. Dan Gottlieb. His program always addressed relational issues, and for me the gift of his wisdom was exceeded only by the warmth and calm of his voice. One day, driving in my car, I tuned in. Dan had a guest on the program who was talking about the new dating scene: the problems of meeting Mr. or Ms. Right on the Internet. A woman called in to say that she was having trouble meeting a decent man, and the guest expert asked if she'd tried this option and that, and she'd tried them all. Then the woman said, "I'm forty-five and I'm getting a little panicky."

The guest stammered and stumbled. Dan jumped in. "What are you afraid of?" he asked.

"Well—just what I said, that I'm not ever going to find somebody."

Dan said, "But what is it that makes you afraid?"

And she said, "Well, just that I'll grow old alone."

"No," Dan said, "that's not what I'm asking you. I'm asking you, *what is it about being alone* that makes you afraid?"

There was a long pause on the line and then the woman said, "Oh, *that*."

Dan said, compassionately, "Yes, *that*." He went on to counsel this woman so wisely. "My hope for you," he said, "is not that you'll simply find a man so this fear will go away, but that you will know this fear, unmask it, welcome it. I want you to open the door and let it in. Let it crawl in bed with you."[2]

Wow. I nearly had to pull the car over and stop. I was almost forty, and I had never before heard anyone speak about fear like that. Maybe it helped in that moment that I knew Dan Gottlieb had been in a car accident and was paralyzed from the chest down. I had seen pictures of him in a wheelchair.[3] I figured this man knew his *merde*. He knew fear. He did not have the heart of a mouse anymore.

When I heard those words, *"I want you to open the door and let it in. Let it crawl in bed with you,"* I was instantly convinced of two things: I could never do that—and it was the only thing to do. I wanted it. (And the thing is, you don't have to know how to do this— you just have to want it.)

Dan Gottlieb's counsel illustrates the radical difference between the strategy of fear, and that of love. Love opens its arms and welcomes what the anxious ego brands as the enemy, the threat. The way to defeat the apparent enemy is not to kill it or throw it down into the cellar, but to befriend it.

There's a wonderful little legend of St. Francis, preserved in that anonymous fourteenth-century Italian book, *The Little Flowers of St. Francis of Assisi.* The story begins with Francis visiting the town of Gubbio. All is not well in the village because a large, fierce wolf is terrorizing the town. He's devouring not only other animals but also human beings. People can hardly go out into the country. When they do, they take weapons, but even fully armed, they can't escape the "sharp teeth and raging hunger of the wolf." The city is locked down. No one dares leave.

Well, Francis decides to go out and meet this wolf, and the people beg him not to walk into certain death. But the story tells how Francis went out armed with nothing but the Sign of the Cross. Sure enough, the wolf comes rushing toward Francis with its fangs bared, and the saint turns and makes the Sign of the Cross in its direction, and the wolf stops.

"Then calling to it, St. Francis said, 'Come to me, Brother Wolf. In the name of Christ, I order you not to hurt me or anyone.'" The wolf lies down at his feet like a lamb.

"Brother Wolf," Francis says, "you have done great harm in this region, and you have committed horrible crimes by destroying God's creatures without mercy." For all these crimes, says Francis, the wolf deserves to die. "But, Brother Wolf, I want to make peace between you and the people, so that they will not be harmed by you anymore, and after they have forgiven you all your past crimes, neither men nor dogs will pursue you anymore."

By nodding its head the wolf gives a sign that it had heard and accepted Francis's word. Whereupon Francis works a deal. The wolf cannot hurt anyone in the town of man or beast, and the townspeople in turn will feed him every day, because he is hungry. The wolf nods.

The two of them walk into the city—imagine the dread of the townspeople. But here comes Francis with the wolf walking by his side. There in the town square with all the people, they seal the pact.

St. Francis holds out his hand to his brother, and the wolf offers his paw.

"From that day, the wolf and the people kept the pact which St. Francis made. The wolf lived two more years, and it went door to door for food. It hurt no one, and no one hurt it.... Then the wolf grew old and died. And the people were sorry, because whenever it went through the town, its peaceful kindness reminded them of the virtues and the holiness of St. Francis."[4]

How do you kill a wolf? By not killing it. You call it Brother Wolf. Because Francis was the only one in Gubbio who had met the wolf within, he was the only one who could deal with the wolf *out there*. His own heart harbored a wolf, and that didn't frighten him anymore. Why? Because the legendary encounter with the wolf in the town square, and the public peace that Francis made between that wolf and the people of Gubbio, was only a repeat performance of an inner reconciliation ceremony, one conducted years earlier in the secret of his own soul.

This counterintuitive way of dealing with fear is not simply a therapeutic program, it's a spiritual undertaking. Therapy is important and good. It can help you conquer your fears and live a more productive life. If you are afraid of open spaces or heights or germs or spiders, there are very good and helpful therapies that can help you manage that fear. But that is not what we are talking about here. The great fear that cripples your soul and keeps you living year after year in that little-*s* self is not finally about anything out there in the world. It is not about all the *objects* of your fears but about the single *subject* of your fears. You.

In 2008 I accompanied my wife to a conference where she was a speaker. The event was held at a nice resort, and speakers could bring a guest and stay free for a week. I was the free guest. Pam was not scheduled to speak until midweek, but on the first night the schedule listed a presentation: "Are You Ready to Stop Letting Fear Control Your Life?" We went.

The presenter began by asking us to think about our fears. She had a clever definition: False Evidence Appearing Real (F.E.A.R.). She urged us to admit our fears—even to imagine a worst-case scenario. Then she asked us to take action. Settle on a specific action we could take to overcome our fear, then break the task into baby steps.

The whole presentation was interactive (which helps when the audience has just had dinner and a few glasses of wine), so she asked us to turn to the person next to us and talk about what our fears feel like. If possible, we were to name one fear.

After giving us some time in groups of two, she called us back into the big group. "Who would be willing to name their fear," the leader asked, "the one you named a moment ago?"

Naturally, people were tentative.

"Come on!" she coached us.

So one man talked about a job situation he was afraid to change; a woman spoke about a relationship she couldn't seem to change. The speaker asked them what specific actions they could take and how they could break the daunting effort into baby steps. The strategy was working. The man with the job worries and the woman with the relationship troubles were clearly going home with a whole new outlook. The crowd was opening up.

"Who else?" the presenter called out.

A woman raised an uneasy hand. "I'm afraid to tell my husband that I need children."

I winced slightly.

"Hmm," the presenter said, "that's a good one."

Awkward pause.

"Yes, any others?"

From the back of the room a man spoke. He was perhaps fifty-five. I had seen him walking to and from sessions with his wife. He struggled to put one foot in front of the other and used a cane.

"I have Parkinson's," he said, "and I am afraid that I'm going to be crippled for the rest of my life."

The pastor in me let out a barely audible groan.

The presenter nodded her head sympathetically. "I'm sorry to hear that," she said, "and I hope you progress well."

The next morning at breakfast, the people at my table were drinking coffee and talking about the night before. They were disappointed in the presenter. She had coaxed us out of our isolation and convinced us to share our fears—a great beginning for the group—but she was unprepared for what had poured out. I said nothing—just listened. People felt sorry for the woman who shared the deeply personal fear of perhaps never having a child and for the poor man who raised a quivering hand to tell us what it felt like to be young and staring down Parkinson's.

For some fears it may work to lay out an action plan, then break it into baby steps. But when we confront our deepest fears, it is not the object that scares the hell out of us, it is the subject. We are afraid of *ourselves*. Or more precisely, it is the little *self* that stands petrified. All suffering, great and small, comes down to this: you are not in control of a situation, and there's almost nothing you can do to change it. That is the ego's worst nightmare.

In the early years most of our problems have solutions, work-arounds. When we feel out of control, we can usually find some way to dispatch our fears into that dark cellar and restore the illusion. But as we age, the loss of control becomes painfully apparent. Cancer, betrayal, depression, cratered careers, lost children, addiction. The fears that attend these moments cannot be broken into baby steps that bring you back to your old self. This is what disturbed the audience that night. They knew this strategy would be of no help to the woman who feared barrenness or the man in dread of the disease wasting his body. You don't make these things go away. You must open the door and let them in, let them crawl in bed with you.

In the movie *Milk,* Harvey Milk receives a death threat. The letter includes a graphic depiction, a stick figure of himself being tortured—shot, stabbed, bleeding. Milk's partner is worried for him, spooked by the letter.

"I'm calling the police!" he says. They're standing in the kitchen. Milk grabs a magnet and sticks the crude drawing to the fridge. His partner is horrified, reaches to take it down. "Don't do that."

Milk replies, "If you put it away in a drawer, it just gets bigger and scarier. Now it's right here, it can't get us."[5]

It's unthinkable in our salad days, but after a few years many people are finally ready to put the little *self* on notice. After years of listening to its nervy, paranoid chatter, you're just done. *Done!* It can't help you anymore, not in phase two where the problems you face can't really be solved. They can only be accepted, understood, held, until they don't threaten you anymore.

Working from an eleventh-century Buddhist meditation, author and teacher Tsultrim Allione has developed a practice she calls "feeding your demons."[6] It's a way of making friends with the things we most want to avoid.

Early-stage spirituality tends to be all about sealing off your demons and creating an ever-more righteous self to present to the world and to God. It's about perfection and control.

Mature spirituality seeks not goodness but wholeness. You want to integrate all the split-off parts of yourself into the fullness of your manhood, your womanhood. You're done choosing which parts of yourself to showcase and which to deep-six. That's the wisdom and energy behind feeding your demons. What if, instead of fighting your demons, you fed them? When we fight them, our demons grow exponentially. But when we invite them in, sit down with them, feed them, offer them a cup of tea, they shrink.

I've counseled many people who manage to serve their demons a spot of tea. A man has lost his job—again—and is terrified of being a failure the rest of his life.

"That old demon of 'failure' is back," I might say. "Tell me about him. What's it like when he gets to work in your head?"

Another man was able to name his persistent demon. He gave it his own middle name, told me all about crazy "Chester" and his predictable antics. I marveled at his fearlessness! And Chester's power over him relented.

I don't have a strategy for befriending your demons, except of course for the three keys to spirituality. Always we return here. I've invited you to become aware of some things you most want to avoid. Because of the work we have done in this Deep Dive passage, it's possible. If you can practice simple awareness, open your heart and *hold it open* (count to ten), you are, as Jesus once said to a fervent seeker, "not far from the kingdom of God."[7]

One last thing. You should not do this work by yourself, and, in fact, you cannot.

Even though much of spiritual formation is necessarily done in solitude, it is not a solitary endeavor. Whenever we turn off the noise and attend to what's really happening below the surface of our lives, we find a peace and quiet that can be utterly delicious, but we also find troubling things. People are sometimes afraid of quiet reflection because they know these fearful things will surface. One man told me with a laugh, "I don't take walks because I have too much to think about." That's why most people undertaking a soul quest seek out a spiritual director. You need someone who's been there, who can tell you that the demons crawling out as soon as you get quiet are (a) quite typical and (b) cannot hurt you. Knowing that makes all the difference. You can sit a moment longer and just observe those critters. This may be a good time, then, to seek out a pastor, a counselor, or a trusted friend.

But there is a more profound sense in which you cannot do this by yourself. When you sit down with your demons, take tea with them, they shrink into this shriveled avatar, something like the pathetic Gollum in *Lord of the Rings*. It is easy to hate that version of yourself, to want it done away with. But, of course, that is not what we're after here. As Robert Bly says, "You don't ever fully get rid of your demons, you just educate them."[8]

In this moment you need a larger, more gracious and merciful Self who can in fact accept and love the little fearful self. Otherwise you will keep rejecting it, reviling it. Healing and wholeness come when you can embrace that sorry little self, knowing that it is you and it always will be. And that it's all right. When this happens, you know it is a miracle *because you could never do this yourself.* This is the work that God does in you. If you allow it.

Now I'm in over my head, telling you, again, a little more than I know.

Deep spirituality is all about holding together two warring things. You are light, and you are darkness. The task is not to fix that by getting rid of your inkiness, but to hold those two opposites in union. Martin Luther, struggling to reconcile the battle engulfing his soul, recognized that he was simultaneously justified and a sinner: *simul justus et peccator.*[9] This is how God saw him, and God did not want him to take that old *peccator* out to the woodshed. Luther called that "works righteousness." Ego. God—not us—is the one who deals with our sin, and his way is always mercy, grace, and acceptance. Luther was finally freed when he let himself fall into the mercy of God. He was not strong enough to hold his two warring selves together, but God was.

This is the mystery I am trying to describe. You need a larger, more gracious and merciful Presence to do this reconciling, this embracing. As you notice that great Self first reaching out a hand of friendship to the fearful, shriveled self, you know you're doing it, and yet you're not. It's some energy coursing through you. If you're doing anything, it's just letting it happen, getting out of its way, not stopping it anymore.

Then it dawns on you that the great Self is actually God-in-you. It is you, and yet it's not you. It is the place where the divine and the human intersect in your soul. The father has leapt off the porch, running headlong down the drive. The prodigal boy has stopped, is standing shamefaced, head down in the middle of the road—you see it all playing out in your own heart. And now the running father falls on the boy's neck, kisses him, embraces the little self, kisses Gollum, and you are finally whole, shadow and all. There is nothing to fear.

THE FOURTH PASSAGE

ARRIVAL TIME: NOW

TWELVE

Dead or Alive

I had seen birth and death but had thought they were different.

—T. S. Eliot

In the last movement you turned inward, spelunking deep into a world hidden beneath the surface of life. There you opened the eye of the heart and began to perceive at another level. What you experienced is a shift in consciousness. It's not simply that what you see looks different, it's that the *I* doing the seeing has changed.

That's what happens when you drop down into this eternal world, when you discover the original self nested like the last Russian doll in your soul's holy of holies. You come back, of course, to the old world clattering away at the surface. You don't have the courage yet to live fully inside that original self, so you still put on the mask that feels more acceptable. But once you've been down there, once you know who you actually are, you are always drawn back to that place where everything shines and you are at peace.

In *Bridge to Terabithia*, two outcast fifth graders, a girl Jess and a boy Leslie, take over part of a nearby forest that can be reached only by a rope swung across a creek. In this country, which they name Terabithia, they are royalty.[1]

I have long loved that image of a rope swinging from a world in which you are an outcast to a world in which you are a king or a queen. Religion holds, as William James said, "that there is an unseen order, and that our supreme good lies in harmoniously adjusting ourselves thereto."[2] Deep faith always assures us that, just a rope swing away from this ugly and pedestrian world set up and controlled by the System, there lies another world in which you are royalty (see 1 Peter 2:9). Going there is not escapist, since that realm is in fact the only real world, and only when you are there are you truly yourself.

When you swing out across the water and fall into this eternal country, you've crossed a time zone. Here everything happens *now*. You've heard about "living in the now." Maybe you thought it was an Eastern religion thing—it is often caricatured as a Zen thing. Let me explain. You don't exactly set out to live in the now. It simply happens whenever you are fully aware. Imagine. You are sitting in a stadium. The running back breaks through the line and punches into the secondary—no one within ten yards! Suddenly what seemed like two-yards-and-a-cloud-of-dust is now a game-breaking gallop. At once you leap to your feet in unison with fifty thousand. *He could go all the way!*

Freeze-frame. In that moment you are not thinking, *How do I look, screaming and jumping like a crazy person?* You are not thinking, *I wonder if I seem successful to my friends or if the car I am driving says the right thing about me.* You don't care about your bad hip or the money you lost in the stock market this morning. You don't care which party is in the White House. You're not pro-life or pro-choice in that instant. You are just wholly present to this moment of pure exhilaration.

Athletes know this moment. They speak of being "in the zone," where you don't think about what you're doing—it just flows out of you. (Often we say of an athlete in a slump, "He's overthinking.") Artists know this moment, when the paintbrush seems to have a will of its own, the words tumble onto the page. Luciano Pavarotti used to speak of his great tenor voice in the third person. It was this gift that came from beyond him, and he was only the channel. Lovers know this moment. Ecstasy is to stand outside yourself, outside time. The reason people pursue extreme sports like mountain climbing, cliff diving, or drag racing is because they focus the body and mind intensely, breathlessly *now*.

Once you cross the time zone into this present moment, you realize how much the conventional world is imprisoned in either the past or the future. The false self is always obsessing about its past, the mistakes it made, the wrongs it suffered, or the glories it won that cannot be allowed to fade away. It is always rushing the future, worrying about calamities that are sure to fall, yet hoping fervently for that great day when vindication finally comes, or windfall or retirement or recognition or plain happiness. The strung-out little self can hardly help itself, lurching wildly from past to future, trying to make it in the conventional world.

But after you've lived like that for thirty or forty years and inevitably come to grief, you understand how living there is a form of death. You don't know that until you've lived inside your true self at least once. Then you know that you are only really alive when you are here, in the present. On either side of *now* is dead space.

Most people live their whole lives on either side of *now*. That's why all religions speak of human beings as dead. The prophet Ezekiel sees the whole of Israel as a field of dry bones.[3] From his palace window, the Buddha sees a corpse and knows it to be the human condition from which he must be freed.[4] In a midnight tête-à-tête Jesus tells Nicodemus that he is dead and must be "born again."[5]

The other, related image for the human plight is of sleepers who need to awaken. The Buddha claps his hands and says, "Wake up!" To no avail Jesus pleads with his disciples to stay awake with him on his last night alive. St. Paul insists, "It is now the moment for you to wake from sleep."[6] It is sleep as death.

What all these prophets say is, you are dead and you don't even know it. You are dead asleep—walking through life, yes, but snoring all the while. The striking image they paint is one we recognize. True spirituality, then, is always about bringing you to life—*now*. But this life is available only to those who know they are dead.

The other evening I was among friends at dinner. We were talking about movies, and I mentioned Christopher Plummer.

"Oh," someone said, "didn't he die recently?" I didn't think so, but it's easy to lose track of celebrities like this. Even if they've bought the farm you still see their pictures, still see them very much alive on the screen.

One man at the table said, "That's easy. We'll just go to deadoraliveinfo.com." Howard whipped out his iPhone and called up the site. I looked curiously over Howard's shoulder as he typed in "Christopher Plummer." Immediately a smiley face popped up. Plummer was alive.

Someone piped up, "What about Kim Novak?" I thought the old-time movie star was long gone, but her name also yielded a smiley face. It wasn't until we entered "Paul Newman" that we got a skull. Dead.

This is what we need—some version of deadoraliveinfo.com for the soul. You have to type in your own name, press Enter. The skull has to pop up. That usually happens against our will. We fall, bottom out, forced to admit that the old life is over.

If you have managed to wreck your so-called life and come to the place of the skull, give thanks. The reason the Twelve Steps work is because the first step begins, "We admitted that we were powerless over alcohol—that our lives had become unmanageable." Powerless. Dead in the water.

Mature spirituality presents one very simple question, and only one: Are you dead or alive? Early-stage religion cannot go there. It will always make the one and only question something like, Are you saved or lost? (Meaning, "Not now, silly, but in the afterlife.") Are you good enough or bad? In or out? Worthy or unworthy? Do you believe or doubt? Have you been baptized or eucharistized or born again or slain in the Spirit—or not?

This stuff makes the ego just salivate. It can spend whole happy days on this hamster wheel.

We have to wrestle with all those questions, which is the necessary task of the first half of life. But at some point—when we sense that we have not yet begun really to live and that we have precious few years to figure this out—suddenly we have no appetite for any of that. Now the only thing that matters is, *What can make me live,* now? *If dead or alive is the question, show me the skull.*

Near the end of his short life, Martin Luther King Jr. said these words:

> You may be thirty-eight years old, as I happen to be. And one day, some great opportunity stands before you and calls you to stand up for some great principle, some great issue, some great cause. And you refuse to do it because you are afraid.... You refuse to do it because you want to live longer.... You're afraid that you will lose your job, or you are afraid you will be criticized or that you will lose your popularity, or you're afraid that somebody will stab you, or shoot at you or bomb your house; so you refuse to take the stand. Well, you may go on and live until you're ninety, but you're just as dead at thirty-eight as you would be at ninety. And the cessation of breathing in your life is but the belated announcement of an earlier death of the spirit.[7]

In other words, for millions and millions the time lapse between death and burial is something like fifty years.

This is why King was so infectiously, fearlessly alive. Because he asked himself, *Dead or alive?*

At four in the morning on April 23, 1849, Fyodor Dostoevsky was rousted from his bed, told to get dressed, arrested, and taken to the headquarters of the secret police. There he was accused of conspiracy against Czar Nicholas (for "printing and distributing works against the government by means of a home lithograph") and sentenced to "the death penalty by shooting." He and scores of other "traitors" were driven to Semenovsky Square in St. Petersburg. There, in deep snow, a firing squad was waiting as a crowd of gawkers gathered around.

The first three condemned men were tied to stakes on the scaffold and blindfolded. Dostoevsky, who was to be in the next three, watched as rifles were raised, cocked, and aimed. Then suddenly an order was given and the guns were lowered. It was the czar's cruel trick of psychological torture: line a man up, blindfold him, and cock the rifle so he can already hear the bullet screaming through the air, crashing through his chest—then drop the weapon and read out a commuted sentence. For Dostoevsky it was four years of penal servitude in Siberia.

The mock execution was a show of imperial might and mercy. But for Dostoevsky it was like dying without dying. He spoke of its profound effect, how his sense of smell and taste were heightened, how he felt the sun's warmth as never before. It was meant as torture, but his moment on the scaffold became a breakthrough moment of existential vividness. He was *alive!*[8]

People at midlife are not so much seeking the meaning of life as they are craving an actual, crackling experience of life. This is not merely a spirituality of peak experiences, seeking wonder and awe climbing Eiger's north face, listening to Mahler's soul-stirring Symphony no. 2, or standing before Michelangelo's *Pietà* in Rome. Those are sublime experiences that can indeed bring us powerfully into the present. But peak experiences—intense feelings of love and well-being—can also be pharmacologically triggered.

The hallmark of authentic spirituality is that it can transmute not only your ecstasy but also your agony. Any fair-weather faith can find a place for your rapture; only the real thing can absorb your suffering and give you back joy. Real faith teaches you to admit your fall and find that you have fallen up; real faith teaches you to acknowledge the death of the self and then find rising within you an infinitely larger Self. Real faith insists that you wake from your sleep and rise from your grave. What you wake to, however, is not a string of peak experiences but simple *experience*. Life as is.

That's why the puny self stays in bed and pulls the covers up over its head. It knows by year forty or fifty (earlier for some) that it can't control all the variables and make it all come out right anymore. The gap between what your life was supposed to be and what it's become creates too much anger and resentment, too much bitterness and apathy. You can't face it.

No, the crippled self cannot imagine waking up. But take heart, the great Self can. It doesn't mind facing life as is because it has already died and found, improbably, that it lives.

This is the secret Martin Luther King Jr. knew. It's what Dostoevsky experienced waiting to climb the scaffold.

It's also what my friend Rachel discovered when a car accident left her for dead. Thirteen years later when I met her, she still needed a cane to walk. "I had to accept the reality that the Rachel I had known for forty-two years was gone forever," she wrote to me. "Everything changed in a second—physical, mental, emotional. A life lost is an incredible experience. For thirteen years my silent prayer has been,

'Lord, I do not know where I am going. This is an unknown life to me, but I have faith that you are here, and this new life must come from you.'"

The heroes and heroines of faith in the second half of life are not the ones who did it all right, lived some charmed life and escaped suffering. They're the ones who could no longer keep the illusion going. They were frogmarched up some scaffold for public humiliation, and they couldn't pretend anymore. They were left for dead in a mangle of metal on the roadside or on a hospital gurney in the cancer ward. They don't just joke about "getting in touch with their mortality," because they have already met death, have already seen their corpses laid out. And they've found, instead of fear and deadness, love and life. Power for bold living.

Once you're dead and you know it, nothing can threaten you anymore. You live now inside a larger life. St. Paul declared, "I have been crucified with Christ." His little self had been nailed, annihilated. "It is no longer I who live, but it is Christ who lives in me" (Galatians 2:19–20).

Dead or alive? That's all that matters now.

THIRTEEN

The Subtracted Life

I have a feeling that my boat has struck, down there in
the depths, against a great thing. And nothing happens!
Nothing...Silence...Waves...
—Nothing happens? Or has everything happened,
and are we standing now, quietly, in the new life?

—Juan Ramón Jiménez, "Oceans"

On January 12, 2007, a young man in jeans, a long-sleeved T-shirt
and a Nationals baseball cap opened his violin case in the
L'Enfant Plaza station of the DC subway system. Morning rush hour
was underway. The man appeared to be an ordinary street musician;
in fact he was the lead player in a social experiment set up by the
Washington Post. What would happen, they wanted to know, if a
musical genius, playing classical masterworks on an exquisite instru-
ment, performed incognito in the subway? Would anybody stop and
listen?

The man in the baseball cap was violinist Joshua Bell, a prodigy
who had quickly risen to stardom. Three days before his underground
debut, Bell was playing Boston's Symphony Hall where a so-so ticket
fetched one hundred dollars, and women swooned over this tousled-
haired heartthrob.

But what would happen if something transcendent were placed
in a plebeian setting where transcendence is least expected? The

experiment's designers asked an expert, Leonard Slatkin, the musical director of the National Symphony Orchestra. Slatkin figured Bell would not be recognized in the setting, but he ventured that at least thirty-five or forty people would recognize the remarkable quality of this great music, and that seventy-five to one hundred people would stop for at least a minute.

At 7:51 Bell lifted the 1713 Stradivarius from its case, struck the chords of the tuning ritual, and dug his bow into Bach's "Chaconne." The acoustics of the open arcade were surprisingly brilliant. Despite the noise and shuffle of hurried commuters, the music rose like a grand soundtrack for this drab scene of rushed contemporary life. Bell delivered a performance worthy of Carnegie Hall, swaying, rising, tossing his head in ecstatic sympathy with J. S. Bach.

It was six minutes before the first person stopped, stood against a wall, and just listened.

Next came Shubert's "Ave Maria." Bell went on to play six masterpieces for forty-three minutes. In all, almost eleven hundred people poured through the station (surveillance cameras tell the tale). Seven people stopped for a minute before hurrying on. Only one woman stopped and listened to an entire piece. She recognized Joshua Bell, not because she was a classical music buff, but because she had come to a free concert Bell had played at the Library of Congress. In the end, 1,089 people sleepwalked right by.[1]

How could this happen? Perhaps a hundred people were the kind who would pay dearly to hear this virtuoso play some gilded concert hall. Even those who didn't especially care for classical music might be expected to stop just because it was an extraordinary live performance. But they didn't. They didn't even seem to notice anything was going on.

The moribund scene of thousands shuffling underground, barely conscious, recalls T. S. Eliot's vision in *The Waste Land,* near the conclusion of "The Burial of the Dead."

Unreal City,
Under the brown fog of a winter dawn,
A crowd flowed over London Bridge, so many,
I had not thought death had undone so many.
Sighs, short and infrequent, were exhaled,
And each man fixed his eyes before his feet.[2]

Eliot's image is more disturbing when you realize that he is echoing Dante's cry of amazement from the pit of the famous *Inferno.* "So long a train of people that I would not have believed death had undone so many."[3] The deadly train that Dante saw in hell, Eliot sees on earth, surging over London Bridge. Modern society, survivors of twin holocausts in two World Wars, had become a procession of the living dead.

This is the human predicament. You are in that procession. I am too. Early on, we're told to get in that long line if we want to "get somewhere in life." It may seem a lifeless parade right now, but, we are assured, it will pay off in the end. So we trudge on. It's the daily grind; it's one more day in the salt mines. Unhappy people doggedly in pursuit of happiness, our inalienable American right. The sad irony, however, is that we are racing after the grand prize...with eyes closed, ears stopped. We couldn't hear Joshua Bell if he were playing three feet in front of us. What else are we missing?

If you can see yourself in that grim march of sleepwalkers, dead to the world, you are—oddly enough—on the verge of something great. It means you are rousing from slumber. As you begin to shake off the narcosis of sleep, you awaken to the richest yet most paradoxical discovery of the spiritual life. Happiness is already here. It's the inherent gift of life itself.

Children are naturally happy (which is why, when the exception proves the rule, it hurts so much). When is the last time you saw a child get up in the morning and go out to pursue happiness? He doesn't. The dawning of a new day is cause for joy in itself. Seeing the dog licking the plates in the dishwasher makes him laugh. He plays with his Cheerios, delighting in a thousand inner tubes floating in a white ocean.

This is what children get in trouble for—having inordinate fun. Children are awake, highly aware, perceiving not only with their senses but also with their minds and souls. We call them sponges because they soak up everything. When they're afraid, you know it; when they're hurting, they cry. Have you noticed how children stop on the sidewalk to pick up a leaf or an ant or a feather? You have to pull them by the hand. "Come on, we don't have time for that. We'll be late."

Imagine walking into L'Enfant Plaza holding a seven-year-old's hand. Try walking past the nice violinist without stopping. You can't. She wants to stop and stare.

Consider Moses, keeping the flock of his father-in-law Jethro on the backside of the desert, minding his business, doing his job. Suddenly he sees a bush on fire, flaming like a giant torch yet unconsumed. Moses says, "I must turn aside and look at this great sight, and see why the bush is not burned up."[4]

I must turn aside! That's what the seven-year-old does instinctively. But the thousands pouring through L'Enfant Plaza, the legions trudging across London Bridge see nothing, notice nothing unusual. They cannot turn aside.

That is us. The August sky is on fire, and we claim to see nothing. A fourteen-year-old boy is standing on the curb, waiting idly for the school bus. You look out the kitchen window and see only that he is there. You miss the morning light that circles his beautiful head like a nimbus. If you could see that your son is lit with divine fire, you would turn aside, find something he "forgot," rush out for one last look at this astonishing avatar who has not even bothered to comb his hair. But scales cover your eyes.

Equally, there are fires of peril. Bushes are burning at work, whole forests are aflame in marriages gone toxic while children fade into smoke, and no one sees a thing, no one turns aside. Eugène Ionesco's Theatre of the Absurd—where polite society types make pleasant small talk while people around them are on fire or are turning into rhinoceroses—seems anything but absurd.

This is what you must do. Step aside, out of the death march. Wake up. In doing so, you reclaim that childlike state of unfiltered awareness, seeing what is plainly before you, taking it all in—the evil and the good. This is not child*ish,* because, like Yeats, you have "cast a cold eye / On life, on death"[5] (more on this in the next chapter). But it is wonderfully childlike. You recover what we might call "original happiness," the natural state that was yours before the cosmos was disenchanted, drained of its inherent power and beauty.

Because in those early days, the world was all right as is. You didn't have to make your own happiness, create your own pleasures. They were just there; you didn't think about it. There was pain, of course—every child knows disappointment and loss—but there was always someone to patch up your broken arm or your broken heart, and you went on living because the good so clearly outweighed the evil. With the odds for good stacked crazy in your favor, you plunged back into life. You didn't know any better.

At some point, though, that good-enough world disappears. A substandard version replaces it: flat, grudging, slightly hostile. It is not for you, it is against you. It holds pleasures, but your task is to steal them. It holds not happiness but the raw materials for happiness; your task is to make it. It does not contain enough beauty, enough recognition, enough money or time or security. You have to make all of that for yourself, and since everyone else is doing the same, there's plenty of competition.

If you try to recall the moment when the enchanted world was lost, your memory may take you back to puberty. That's when four quarts of hormones pour into your bloodstream. Suddenly you have needs and desires. You are powerfully directed toward something else, something far away from here. You feel the urge to merge, and it drives you in search of some "other." You are hungry for love, sex, progeny, self-esteem, recognition, a place in the sun. Eros sends you on a relentless quest that abates only in the middle passage, and often drives a man or woman into their sixties and seventies still seeking what's "missing," what will fill the void inside.

Eros fuels more than just the adolescent sexual urge. It's the energy that drives us to achieve, to master our profession, to reach our distant goals. Without this urgent passion, we would be listless and useless. But Eros is a blinding power. In its throes we seek only the fulfillment of our desire: to right terrible wrongs, to attain perfection, to achieve some public good for which our name will be remembered. To all else we are oblivious, blind to this present moment.

In this state the world is not all right as is. It is broken and needs to be repaired (which is where heroes and heroines are created). Life must be forced to render its goods; it does not yield happiness of itself. The present world is what must be overcome, transcended! Happiness lies somewhere over the rainbow. We are all like Adam and Eve, who live in Paradise and wake one day to find that they are naked and hungry, panting like hell to escape heaven. The good stuff is out there somewhere, and God is keeping it from them.

And so we spend most of our lives like racing greyhounds, chasing a fake rabbit in circles. The System presents happiness as an object that is outside the self and must be pursued, run down, captured. Thomas Merton called it "organized despair." It never works.

But before you realize this, you have to pursue happiness. You have to chase that stupid rabbit until you're sick and tired. No one can tell you about this; you have to experience it for yourself. Then it finally dawns on you. The thing you truly seek is already yours; you've always had it. It's comical, really. Like scouring the whole house in search of your glasses, then finding them atop your head.

Augustine—long before he became "St. Augustine"—chased a lot of fake rabbits in a lifestyle famously louche. It all ended in despair. Then came those well-known words, "Late have I loved you, O Beauty, so ancient and so new, late have I loved you! You were within, but I was outside, seeking there for you."[6] The object of his intense search was, in fact, not an object out there at all; it was within, his true self.

"Late have I loved you." We all come late to this party. We don't get here by succeeding, getting what we want. We get here precisely by losing the prize, being stripped, standing empty-handed. The things we think will make us happy have to be taken away.

The strangest rule of spiritual growth is that it begins against your will. People in Twelve Step programs know this best. You undergo the stripping, and when you've endured the pain without resorting to your usual escape routes, you find a new kind of joy. It's the kind that only comes from nothing. It's a happiness that is not contingent on any *thing;* it just *is.* You didn't gain it, and you can't lose it.

This happiness has nothing to do with your circumstances. Mother Teresa, living and working in what you and I would consider hell, somehow knew she had a happiness that could not be taken away.[7] Or as my Great Plains mother used to say, "Blessed be nothing."

When you reach this state, the good-enough world returns. You begin to grasp the paradoxical upside-downness of human life. The more you lose, the better this life gets. Why? Because each "loss" returns you one step closer to original happiness, to that blessed nothing. "Art," says Picasso, "is the elimination of the unnecessary."[8] The same applies to happiness.

Meister Eckhart, the fourteenth-century mystic, says, "The soul grows by subtraction rather than by addition."[9] After all the years of addition—acquiring things, experiences, titles, even people—the whole calculus shifts. Now it's about subtraction, shedding, letting go. It's not just getting rid of *things* (at some point all of us will downsize whether we choose to or not), it's also a conscious release of our *will to happiness*—by our own cunning and strength, charm and good looks. Our deepest joy and pleasure, we now know, is not anything we can chase. In fact, the more we pursue it, the further it recedes.

"Perfection is finally attained," writes Antoine de Saint-Exupéry, "not when there is no longer anything to add but when there is no longer anything to take away, when a body has been stripped down to its nakedness."[10]

Being stripped down to its nakedness scares the living daylights out of the nail-biting little self. Because there is nothing there, it seeks desperately for things to pour into that void. Love, affirmation, sex, more affirmation, career, a stunning career, a house, a chateau featured in *Architectural Digest,* children, Ivy League children—it never ends.

Your little self will never consent to this stripping down to its nakedness. That is why you need faith and trust. You cannot do this on your own. And you don't need to. You need only pray for the grace to cooperate with the mystery at work within you.

All of this happens, as I noted, against your will. Once you come out of the halfway turn and head home, life naturally begins the subtraction process. Your physical powers slacken, and your children leave you behind. The company lets you go early. The two of you stand in an empty big house. All of this *will happen*. You can fight it, or you can let it take you where you need to go; let the greater Self emerge, the one who welcomes the loss of all things that hide its inherent beauty, the one who lives not in fear but in the power of love, the one who is not afraid to die. When you cooperate with the mystery at work within, you get a little taste of holy joy. You endure some loss and you find, after the sadness, that it's not just okay—it's better this way!

The feverish pursuit of happiness is over, and a calm sense of acceptance descends. After all those years of chasing the ebb tide, you watch the waters turn. You sit on the beach and let them roll over you. Little pleasures become huge. Plain things shine once more. You fall in love again. The world is not just good enough, it is gorgeous. Everything you need is right here, right now. With Emily Dickinson, you want to exclaim, "To live is so startling, it leaves but little room for other occupations."[11]

FOURTEEN

Dropping My Demands

I demand more than happiness! I demand euphoria!

—Calvin of *Calvin and Hobbes*

I f it were easy to live in the *now*, everyone would do it.

Nearly everyone comes to a moment when the question "Dead or alive?" elicits a stirring will to live. And after people have chased the bluebird of happiness and ended up depressed, they are ready to find the joy sitting unregarded in their lap. But how do you actually *do* that?

By now you already know. It's the three keys to spiritual life. You need to become aware—and stay aware—of the unspoken expectations you have of life. It is easy to see the unreal expectations of others, but not our own.

A few months ago I got a call from Roger, a man in anguish. His best friend had just committed suicide, and Roger was sitting with the dead man's widow and her three children. It was a horrible moment, he said, made worse by the ghoulish publicity.

"It's already been picked up by the *Wall Street Journal*," Roger said. His best friend was a successful businessman and philanthropist. "Just Google his name," he told me sadly.

Later I did. I could hardly believe that a man who had been everywhere, done it all, achieved prowess and renown could come to such an end. I kept staring at his birth date, a few years later than my own.

Everyone can see in this tragedy the terrible mismatch between what life offered one man and what he demanded to be happy. What is more difficult is spying the mismatch between what life offers us this very morning and the expectations that are already set in our heads when we get out of bed. What will have to happen before this day can be called good?

This is especially tricky for people who live in the First World. We are born with assumptions that are simply unrealistic, the bar set so high that failure is inevitable. John Cheever, whose stories reveal the shadowed hearts of Ivy League heirs, once observed, "The main emotion of the adult Northeastern American who has all the advantages of wealth, education, and culture is disappointment."[1]

What you must learn in order to be not dead but alive—*in this moment*—is to drop your demands. First bring those unconscious requirements to awareness, then drop them.

We could examine a thousand little demands. If it's a rainy day, you're bummed. If you hit the *long* red light at the first corner on your way to work, you're angry. If your boss (who never compliments anybody) doesn't thank you for that good quarterly earnings report at 9:00 a.m., you're going to be grousing all day. Unless your wife loses those seven pounds again, you will not look at her as beautiful.

Or, we could just cut to the chase.

The problem is not all those little ultimatums; it is the big one: reality is just not keeping up its end of the bargain, and we insist that it get its act together and start performing.

People often speak or write about living in the present as if it were only sunshine and roses. In fact, in this moment you encounter plain, un-spun reality.

When we inhabit this instant, all we have is *this*. The dog is sleeping on the sofa, the gutter is dripping, the laundry is piled in the hallway, the ebony elephant sculpture you brought back from Kenya stands utterly still on the end table. This is it. Later on perhaps someone will come home and stories will be told, maybe you will enjoy the mushroom ravioli in the fridge and open a bottle of wine. There may be a good show on television. But right now this is all there is.

The happiness of this moment is pure and simple, but so is its suffering, its boredom. We all want the happiness but not the suffering. We feel entitled to the former and exempt from the latter. That is our basic problem with reality and the reason why we are not willing to accept what simply is. It does not meet our standards, and we intend to change it!

That's why although it is fashionable to speak of "living in the now," most people do not really want to. Frankly, they don't like *now*. I know I don't. Not unless I have consciously decided that today, right now, I will love what is.

In this chapter I want you to see that big ultimatum—learn to start seeing it every day, putting it back on the front burner of consciousness after it inevitably slides to the back. In the passage after this one, we will learn some of the spiritual practices—like meditative prayer and absolute forgiveness—that help us, day in and day out, to release the wildly unrealistic expectations of life that set us up for disappointment. But right now we need to get a good long look at that one big ultimatum.

In the early years we demand something better of life. *I don't like the way you're operating, and I demand big changes.* We imagine that we can manage the darkness, make the pain go away. We can cure our woundedness, protect others from suffering, right every wrong.

After we have lived a few more years, however, we know it can't be done. Once that realization sinks in, either things get better or they get a lot worse. Once the little self figures out (as absurd as it seems even to say) that it cannot make the universe snap to attention and change its course, that it cannot change the very nature of reality, it has no choice but to make up its own world. The puny self will not live in a world where "God" cannot seem to do his job and banish darkness, exile disease, and dispel all suffering. It will not have it! It will not live in the real world anymore, not where light and darkness commingle, not where joy cannot be sundered from sorrow.

Human life teeters on this moment. Because once you reject the world as it really is, you are self-condemned to live like a wraith in some shadow realm. The only way to stay alive is to embrace the world—the whole thing, in all its contradiction and benediction. Or, to say it another way, your only salvation in this moment is to admit that you cannot change the world, that the one who needs to be changed is you.

This modern parable sums it up.

A battleship assigned to a training squadron had been at sea on maneuvers in heavy weather off the California coast for several days. As night fell, the captain noticed the patchy fog and decided to remain on the bridge. Shortly after dark, the lookout on the wing of the bridge reported, "Light. Bearing on the starboard bow."

"Is it steady or moving astern?" the captain asked.

The lookout replied, "Steady, captain," which meant the battleship was on a collision course with something.

The captain called to the signalman, "Signal that ship. You are on a collision course. Advise you alter course 20 degrees."

Back flashed the answering signal, "Advisable that you change course 20 degrees."

The captain said, "Send another message. I am a senior captain. Change course 20 degrees."

"I am a seaman second class," came the reply. "Change your course at once."

The officer was furious. He spat out, "I am a battleship. Change your course 20 degrees."

The flashing light replied, "I am a lighthouse."

If the captain is sensible, of course, he will turn his ship. But that is a rare feat for most men and women, who prefer to crash heroically into the rocks. We insist that the oncoming lights in our lives are a threat. They signal that we must change course, but we do not acknowledge their authority. *I am the master of my fate. I am the captain of my soul.*

When the famous British unbeliever Bertrand Russell was asked by a reporter from *Look* magazine in 1953 what it would take to shake his atheism, Russell replied that he would believe in God "if I heard a voice from the sky predicting all that was going to happen to me in the next 24 hours."[2]

Startlingly silly. Like a small child. Russell's demand—to know the future—comes straight from the needy, anxious self. "If you were any kind of decent God," it pouts, "you would satisfy my need to control time and destiny."

Instead God replies, "I know, Bertrand, I know. Take my hand. How can I explain this to you? I know nothing of the future. Because *I AM*, I know only the eternal present. Let's go for a walk, the two of us—now."

Known as the Great Agnostic of the nineteenth century, Robert Ingersoll sulked that if he were God he would have made health contagious instead of disease.[3] Let me tell you: if you go through life blaming the Architect of the universe for contagious diseases, you are running backward up a down escalator, stumbling, falling, and cursing the Idiot who designed the system. You might as well spit nails in the wind.

In *The Brothers Karamazov,* Dostoevsky has Ivan blurt out, "I don't accept this world of God's. Although I know it exists, I don't accept it at all. It's not that I don't accept God, you must understand, it's the world created by Him that I don't and cannot accept."[4]

Ivan's adamant objection is yours and mine. We all say no to suffering. It is suffering that causes the mad human exodus from reality. As Peter De Vries laments, "Why [is] that question mark twisted like a fishhook in the heart."[5] Unless we can find some way to contain suffering—some way to know that it is part of the good creation of God—we cannot be fully human. We will inevitably reject the only life there is. *I will go on living, but I do so under protest.* As Woody Allen remarked, "If God exists, I hope he has a good excuse."[6]

Now I am barefoot on my knees. Any time we speak of human suffering, the shoes come off: this is holy ground. To embrace anguish and heartache, to know that it belongs—somehow!—in God's good creation is a profound mystery. Unless you're one of Job's friends, you don't walk up to someone doubled over in grief and suggest that he might want to embrace his suffering. All we can do, especially for young people, is to hold them and add our tears to theirs, pray that the pain will not break their spirit and lead to bitterness. Because if we can hold on, without demanding explanations or reparations, without either anger or unearned acceptance, the peace that passes understanding can descend. It is wholly a gift of grace wrought by love, but it can descend. And when it does, we can sing or sigh that hymn,

> When peace like a river attendeth my way,
> When sorrows like sea billows roll,
> Whatever my lot, Thou hast taught me to say,
> It is well, it is well, with my soul.[7]

The pain does not go away, but the heart opens, it seems, just a little wider so that the agony slips inside and sits next to our bright joy, and it is somehow all right, both of them, together.

Now I am off my knees and telling you what I regret to know. Most people do not get here. They refuse to let the agony inside. Their hearts are reserved only for bright joy.

All great religion shows you how to hold your suffering, how to answer that question mark twisted like a fishhook inside you. Moses lifted up a bronze serpent in the wilderness and commanded the snake-bitten, dying Israelites to look not *away* from their fear but precisely *at it:* "Look...and live!"[8] The central icon of Christianity is a God-Man on a cross. The First Noble Truth of Buddhism is: Life is suffering.

There is no answer. All you can do is drop your demands and drop to your knees, trust that the great *God-Self* within you can hold the pain until you can breathe again. When you allow this to happen, when you say yes to life, to reality, you become a full human being. "We are healed of our suffering," according to Marcel Proust, "only by experiencing it to the full."[9]

This, then, is your moment, quivering with outrage and opportunity. Now is the time to open your heart and let the enemy in. Do it now to save yourself any more self-inflicted pain.

I have taped these words of Thomas Merton to the wall over my desk: "The truth that many people never understand, until it is too late, is that the more you try to avoid suffering the more you suffer, because smaller and more insignificant things begin to torture you, in proportion to your fear of being hurt."[10]

I remember meeting Eric in the cloister outside church one Sunday. He was out of work, stressed, his wife was having panic attacks. I knew all this because he had come to talk with me regularly over the last year. I greeted Eric casually and asked how he was doing.

"Things are fine," he said happily.

I leaned in, slightly startled. The job? I queried. The stress, the panic attacks—some major breakthrough?

"No," Eric replied with a smile, "we're still dealing with all that. I've just decided it's okay."

The ultimatum is rescinded. The demand is dropped. This is the great passage to wisdom that enables us to live in this present, mixed-bag moment. It happens when we finally know that the world is all right just the way it is, pain included. Instead of rejecting legitimate suffering, we turn and embrace it.

Theologian Hans Urs von Balthasar helps us make that turn. "The wound which we find at the heart of everything," he tells us, "is finally incurable. Yet we still must try! And, in fact, we are driven to try!"[11]

If you don't try, you become a cynic. You have to believe that wound can be made all right—and it can, but all of your curative efforts must fail in order for the realization to fall like Newton's apple: the wound at the heart of life can never be cured, it can only be healed. And there is a difference between a cure (when all the symptoms go away for good) and a healing (when they don't all go away and not always for good).

After raising Christ from the dead and granting him a "glorified" body, God could not find a way to remove the five wounds. Our healing comes not when our scars are taken away, but when our wounds are plunged into the loving heart of God. You can't figure this out in your head. You only know it when the cure you cry out for never comes and deep healing settles instead.

When you drop your demands for a better world than the one God created, you realize that you don't have to fix yourself and all those other, faulty people; you don't have to save the world. It doesn't mean there isn't injustice and evil, poverty and cruelty and war, nor that God wills it and will allow it to stand. It just means you find out who's God and who's not.

Roger Rosenblatt learned this the hard way.

Walking in Washington, D.C., one afternoon, I came upon a baby rabbit that had been separated from its mother. It was sitting stone-still on a patch of grass outside an apartment house, stunned, and was waiting to die. At home, I tried to feed it milk, using an eye-dropper. It would not swallow. I called a veterinarian. He told me the rabbit would die no matter what I tried because without its mother it was literally scared to death, too frightened to save itself. I could not accept such a diagnosis. I kept trying to feed the thing, to coax it to life—which is to say, to be something other than itself. At one point I grew furious, gripped its frail body in my hands and called out, "Live! Damn it!" But it would not. And after some hours things went as the vet said they would.[12]

That is the ego screaming, "Live! Damn it!" It always hides behind our best intentions.

The world is full of egoic people who cannot stop "doing good." Yet when they are met with opposition or failure, they turn angry and self-righteous and whiny because, quite simply, they are not getting their way. Rabbis and pastors and charity heads burn out at alarmingly high rates because they are going to make this thing "Live! Damn it!"

Philosopher Alan Watts points out the pitfalls of trying to save the world before you have acknowledged how deeply your ego is invested in all this. "Many of the troubles going on in the world right now are being supervised by people with very good intentions whose attempts are to keep things in order, to clean things up, to forbid this, and to prevent that. The more we try to put everything to rights, the more we make fantastic messes."[13]

The people who are best prepared to change the world are, in fact, those who have confronted their own egos and no longer need to impose them on the world. These are finally the people who can cooperate with the Creator and Sustainer of it all, who can—like Martin Luther King Jr., Dorothy Day, Paul Farmer—truly change the world because they have allowed *themselves* to be changed. When asked what was wrong with the world, G. K. Chesterton replied, "I am."

For centuries the mystics of every tradition have gone hoarse trying to tell us that everything is right just the way it is. But we would not hear it. After all, we're Americans. Our national creed is self-improvement, and we have repurposed all the world's religions—based solely on unmerited grace, love, and surrender—into ritualized self-help societies. By God, we are going to improve ourselves; our children are going to do even better; we are going to get rid of our sins if it's the last thing we do; and, so help us God, we are going to clean up the world, establish peace by righteous force of arms, cure cancer, and abolish hunger by the metric ton of wheat. Don't try to tell us everything is okay. The simple declaration that things are all right as is defies reason. Anybody can see things are a mess.

When we learn to accept things as they are, we are freed from the need to be the savior of the world and can humbly allow God to work through us. (More on faith in action in the final passage.) But the only faith the little self can gin up is a commitment to hard work on behalf of the Kingdom come. If we all get busy and clean things up, God may yet make an appearance.

What the mystics show us is a joy, a peace, a blessedness that only God can bring and that flourishes in the midst of mess.

You probably know those sublime words of Julian of Norwich, "All shall be well, and all shall be well, and all manner of thing shall be well."[14] What many of us don't know is their context.

Julian was born in fourteenth-century England during the days of the Black Death. The bubonic plague erupted in Norwich three times during Julian's life. Almost nothing is known of this woman's life, but because she never mentions a family, some have reasoned that Julian was one of many women who had lost husband and children to one of the plagues. In addition to the pall of death, this was an epoch of poverty, heavy taxes, famine, unemployment, political unrest, war with France, religious hatreds, and persecution.

In May 1373 at the age of thirty-one, Julian was infected with the plague. Last rites were administered on the fourth day of her illness, and on the seventh day her mother mercifully closed her daughter's eyelids. It was in this moment that Julian felt a surge of life within her plague-wracked body. She was transported into heavenly realms where she received visions of Christ, sixteen in all. To a turbulent, death-besotted world Julian spoke of life and hope. Her visions reveal a God vast in patience, compassion, and love.

By all modern accounts this should not be possible. How could a woman living in a Dürer woodcut of hell utter some of the most sublime words of hope and joy in the English language? I don't know, but it's clear that her confidence was not negated by suffering. Her world was not what we would consider tolerable, and she had no evidence that it was going to change anytime soon. What's more, she had absolutely no discernible calling to rise up, heroically, and fix the situation. Her life and joy, happily, did not depend on her. It was founded on God, in the fire of whose love all suffering was transmuted into glory.

Dame Julian was not waiting for a better world in which to rejoice. Bubonic plague and high taxes notwithstanding, "All shall be well, and all shall be well, and all manner of thing shall be well."

This is where we lay down our ultimatums. It's where we stop telling reality a thing or two and start listening, stop the finger wagging and the fist shaking. It's when the light of awareness reveals all the conditions we place on life. *I will not be happy unless...* Once you begin to see how your petulant demands are keeping you from enjoying the only world God has ever made, the only life on offer, you can drop those demands.

Then you can live *now.*

UNCONDITIONAL

SURRENDER

FIFTEEN

Tidal Turn

> The world for which you have been so carefully
> prepared is being taken away from you by the grace
> of God.
>
> —Walter Brueggemann

The blessing that comes of "Dropping My Demands" leads perfectly to the next passage. The dropping, the relinquishing, is just the right exercise for the work of Unconditional Surrender. Here, in the paradoxical ways of the soul, we learn to let go of what is being taken away, to dive when we are falling, to surrender when we have already lost the struggle.

Second-half spirituality is characterized by this reversal, this tidal turn. This isn't something you *decide* or *do* exactly. You don't decide that now would be a good time for the sea to pour back in upon itself and expose the shore, the rocks, and stranded shells. You surely don't *do* it. What we're sketching with broad strokes is the great cycle of life. All you can do is be aware of it. Sense the tidal shift and know what you must do in response.

According to the poet William Meredith, the worst that could be said of a man is that he did not pay attention. Did not notice, in this case, that the gibbous moon is wasting to a sliver, and the seas are slowly draining from the shore.

Annoyed by the hyperreligious who attended to the minutiae of moral and religious life but missed the great urgency of the moment, Jesus says, "You have a saying that goes, 'Red sky at night, sailor's delight; red sky at morning, sailors take warning.' You find it easy enough to forecast the weather—why can't you read the signs of the times?"[1]

Latter-stage faith begins to know these times. It knows, especially at this stage of life, when the tide is going out, when things are being taken away. It senses the season and goes—as we say—with the flow.

When I came to my first church fresh out of seminary, I was fortunate to be mentored by an older priest who was already semi-retired, in his late sixties. Fred used to tell me over and over how important it was to "be carried by life." He must have seen me arduously pushing my way upriver and felt sorry for me. I never understood what old Fred was trying to tell me.

It all made sense, though, some years later, when my friend Barry told me how he and his new bride nearly drowned on their honeymoon. "Remember how when you're dating," he said, "you don't exactly tell the truth? Well, Liz told me that she loved the beach and swimming, and so I said I did too. We got married and went to North Carolina on our honeymoon. The first day, we're on the beach, just playing in the water, when we feel a strong undertow. Nags Head in June is infamous for its riptides. We're being sucked out to sea.

"Liz started churning for the shore, and called to me, 'Come on!'

"That's when I told the truth. I screamed, 'I don't really know how to swim!'"

Barry could only tread water; he was frantically trying to keep his head above the waves. Liz swam over and held his arm as they dog-paddled together.

"We waved our arms and yelled at the people on the beach," Barry said, "but no one saw us." They were being pulled farther and farther from shore. Gradually exhaustion overtook them. They were astonished to realize that they were both thinking the same thing. *We're going to drown.*

"Finally I said to Liz, 'You can swim. You go on in. I love you.'

"But she said, 'I'm not leaving you. Either we live together or we die together.'

"So we decided to die together. We turned over on our backs and floated, panting at first until we could get our breath. We closed our eyes and held hands. We let the current pull us out until, we thought, eventually we would go under."

Then after a while, Barry said, they felt sand under their heels. The current had brought them back to shore.

Barry's story proves riptide wisdom: don't fight it. Just let it carry you, and go with it. Unfortunately, though, his tale also proves how deadly our instincts are in that moment. Because fighting your way through is so incredibly powerful and effective in the early years, you almost always resort to that fighting spirit—even when the tide has shifted, when the times have changed so that now fighting is the worst thing you could do.

Hence the importance of this passage, Unconditional Surrender. Somewhere midfaith we have to learn how to let go and be carried. This is the essence of faith—utter trust—and yet its full understanding falls to this season. Until now, faith has mostly meant working hard and keeping our fingers crossed. Now, however, we learn total surrender, and that learning is forced upon us. It comes, as we have already noted, against our will. Our only response is to let it happen. Let go.

A friend and colleague from my Chicago days once told me of her moment of forced surrender. It was while sitting on her living room sofa, Jean said, that she felt the grace and mercy of God on the most frightening day of her life. It came, she said, when she cried out for help because there was nothing else to do.

It began with a phone call. Her brother-in-law was calling to say he had just talked to Jean and Michael's son, Ryan. It was Ryan's freshman year of college in Texas. He "had not sounded right at all."

Michael got on the phone. Ryan was in very bad shape. Irrational, distressed, paranoid. Had the medication for the depression that showed up in high school stopped working? Or was something far worse emerging? Within twenty-four hours Michael was on a plane from Chicago to Dallas. Michael got Ryan out of his dorm room, took him to a hotel, laid him on a bed, wrapped his arms around him, and held him all night. The next day began a series of phone calls and meetings with psychiatrists in a desperate attempt to diagnose and address Ryan's condition. Finally they ended up at a major hospital in the office of the head of psychiatry.

The doctor put it bluntly. "This young man must be hospitalized. He is a danger to himself. To keep him safe, you must commit him. Now."

Michael was horrified and confused. Ryan, by now sedated with multiple meds, sat silent. Then, out of nowhere, came Ryan's voice. "Dad, I want you to hear. Try very hard, Dad. I am begging you. Do not put me in the hospital. I want to stay with you. Please, Dad. I am begging you. Hear me, please."

Michael listened. Then, bucking every instinct to the contrary, he took Ryan out of that office and back to the hotel room. He called Jean, back in Chicago. She assured him that he alone was the best judge of what was right for their son. She trusted him completely.

Ryan was weeping; Michael was weeping. Jean was weeping over the phone. "We prayed on the phone," Jean said. "We prayed separately. Please God, what do we do? Give us guidance. Make your will known, please!"

That night, Michael and Ryan boarded a plane for Chicago.

"So they came home," Jean said, "and we began a three-month journey through hell. We witnessed our son plunge into the deepest, darkest, loneliest despair that a human can experience. We took turns standing watch over him hour by hour, day by day. Michael was heroic. Awesome. Heartbroken and terrified, he was the one who took Ryan to doctor after doctor, trying to find the right one and the right medication.

"After a month or two, we thought we'd found the right doc. He spoke with great authority. Ryan trusted him. The problem was, we would have to be patient. The medication would take a month or two to work, if it was going to work at all.

"Meanwhile, Ryan's terrible pain continued. It was grueling to be at home 'on watch.'

"One night, Michael was late in relieving me. I had been 'on call' with Ryan for hours. I was sitting on the sofa in the living room, directly under Ryan's bedroom. I was beside myself, discouraged, weepy, annoyed, frustrated, terrified. I wanted to *get out of there*!

"Then I heard Ryan upstairs. He began to literally pound the walls and moan like an animal. Deep groans came through the ceiling. The walls shook. At that moment, I thought my heart would break.

"Then I heard Ryan's door open. He began to descend the staircase. *Oh no, what now?* I thought. *Please God, help me.*

"Ryan rounded the corner, looking like a wild, wounded animal. He threw himself into my lap on the couch, clinging to me, crying, 'Mom, I can't bear it one more second. I can't. It hurts too much. I can't bear it.'

"We began to sob together, our arms wrapped tightly around each other, crying and crying. It felt as though the ground would sink beneath us. We were one cry, one prayer, one being, one pain. In that moment I fell into the suffering, died into it. All I could whisper was, 'Help!'

"Then Ryan lifted his head off my lap and just looked into my eyes. We sat there for a second, stunned, soaking wet. He said, 'Mom, what was *that*?'

"I said, with a smile, maybe even a laugh, 'I don't know. It was Something, though.'

"A time of silence passed.

"And then, in a perfectly normal voice, Ryan said, 'Hmm, I think I'll get a sandwich.' He jumped off the couch and headed toward the kitchen, normal as can be, like any other kid. There was a lightness; I don't know how or why, but it was there. Present. From that night onward, Ryan got better."

Jean's experience illustrates the classic spiritual experience of letting go, because it happens when we can do nothing else. The ego would love to make letting go some great performance, one more spiritual accomplishment, but the most we can do is allow what is happening to happen. We don't know it is an act of faith until it is over. Only then can we look back and see that when we could not hold it any longer, another Presence was there, holding us. That Presence is always there, in fact, and especially when the egoic self is collapsing, it will surge into consciousness and seek entry into our lives. The beauty of amazing grace is that we are only able to welcome that Presence when we are finally powerless to refuse it.

It may seem contradictory that grace comes only when it cannot be refused because we have already noted that every movement of God within our lives waits upon our will. Like Mary, who was overshadowed (we could say *overpowered*) by the Most High,[2] but who still had to say yes for the divine plan of incarnation to be conceived within her, you and I must also say yes. We must consent at every moment to God's will and way in our lives. Thus it is always possible to be overshadowed, overpowered—as Jean was, as Barry and Liz were—and still fight the divine will to the dead last. The paradoxical balance we seek, then, is to cooperate with what is overpowering us. To know the times and seasons. To sense what is approaching at every stage of life, to say yes to what is coming anyway, bidden or unbidden.

Thomas Keating, the Trappist monk and architect of the Centering Prayer movement, speaks of four consents that God asks of us at different stages of life. First, as children, God asks us to consent to "the basic goodness of our nature with all its parts." This goodness is not what we can accomplish with these gifts of our bodies, imagination, memory, language—but merely the gifts in themselves.

Then in adolescence, God asks us to accept "the full development of our being, by activating our talents and creative energies." When our bodies come fully into man- and womanhood and we find mastery over them, when we develop deeper human relationships, take responsibility for our lives and vocations, and respond to the awakening of our sexual energies, God invites us to say yes to these changes and walk courageously into the next act of life.

Of adulthood, Keating writes,

> God invites us to make a third consent: to accept the fact of
> our nonbeing and the diminutions of self that occur through
> illness, old age and death. The passing of a friend or relative,
> or some accident, may invite us to reflect on our own death....
> Acceptance of our own nonbeing is not directed to the morbid
> side of death but rather to the consequences of dying: the
> letting go of everything we love in this world, whether persons,
> places, or things.[3]

This is the passage to adulthood: accepting the fact that we are dying, and have been since we were born, by letting go of everything we love in this world. It leads us finally to the fourth consent: to be transformed. This may seem a simple consent, Keating notes, but because transforming union requires the death of the false self it is difficult to say yes.

This letting go is something we can and must speak of with children, adolescents, and young adults. But its full understanding—along with the blessed knowledge of death—is reserved for a later time. If we are awake and aware, if we are attuned to the seasons, sensing the "signs of the times," we will know when the "diminutions of self that occur through illness, old age, and death" are now occurring, and when it is time to let go.

Accepting the "diminution of self" will frighten anyone who knows nothing of the little self. When you know that it is only that egoic character that is being dismantled, the fear abates. Indeed, you come to know in your own experience this inverse ratio: the more your self is diminished, the more your Self expands. We see this especially in holy souls of advanced age. As their physical powers wane, they seem to possess a more distilled and concentrated inner energy. They are more spiritually alive and potent now than they were thirty or forty years ago. We see it too in those of any age whose physical bodies are incapacitated (the likes of a Stephen Hawking, a blind Milton, or a deaf Beethoven) and whose tragedy enables them—forces them, in some sense—to pour all their energies into that inner Self. These will tell you how their loss became their gain.

Once you experience the oxymoronic power of your own diminution, you are onto something. You are almost fearless. You are love-driven. Wide open. Vulnerable. What used to threaten you now empowers you.

In Genesis 32 the patriarch Jacob famously wrestles with an angel. The struggle happens at the most terrifying moment in Jacob's life. He is, we could say, a middle-aged man. In his youth, he used his cunning to steal his elder brother Esau's birthright and paternal blessing.

For these family crimes he had to flee—or face the wrath of his brother who had sworn to kill him.

Jacob steals away to his uncle Laban's place in Haran. He has to work fourteen years for her, but he gets a gorgeous wife, Rachel. He's like an ancient Michael Milken or Ivan Boesky—he swindles his way to a fortune. Meanwhile he has eleven children. He's an incredible Bronze Age success. But after all these years, Esau is coming for him. With four hundred men.

A wealthy man, Jacob tries to buy his way out of death by sending his servants on ahead to meet his brother with a livestock gift equivalent to four or five million shekels. To avoid total annihilation, he splits his family and all their household staff into two parties and sends them over the river Jabbok ahead of him. There on the riverbank he is left totally alone, a man who got everything he ever wanted by hook or by crook but who now feels the knife at his throat. There by the river appears an angel—a thinly veiled Hebrew avatar of God—who wrestles with him till daybreak.

Because heavenly beings can work only under conditions of darkness (which ought to tell us something hopeful of the soul's dark night), the fight is called because of lightness. The sun is coming up, and the angel is out of time to finish off this mortal. In divine desperation, he touches Jacob's hip and—*pow*—pulls it from its socket. In his excruciating pain, Jacob can no longer fight. Now like a battered heavyweight he hugs his opponent close to avoid the roundhouse knockout.

"I will not let you go," Jacob says, "until you bless me." There the angel blesses Jacob and changes his name to Israel, "Triumphant with God."[4]

As Jacob is going down, he holds on to his overpowerer. His blessing-in-defeat is the classic story of this vital paradox. When he senses that he is up against a force so powerful it can either destroy him or divinize him, Jacob knows when to let the fight go and how to do the unthinkable: fall into the power that threatens to destroy you. Fall in and hold on. He knows what James Fowler calls "the sacrament of defeat."[5]

In his poem, "A Man Watching," Rainer Maria Rilke recalls the story of Jacob contending with the angel, and then closes with these lines.

> Whoever was beaten by this Angel
> (who often simply declined the fight)
> went away proud and strengthened
> and great from that harsh hand,
> that kneaded him as if to change his shape.
> Winning does not tempt that man.
> This is how he grows: by being defeated, decisively,
> by constantly greater beings.[6]

Having discovered the ruin of "winning," the second-half soul begins to understand this sensational mystery: after a certain point we grow only "by being defeated, decisively, by constantly greater beings."

SIXTEEN

The Surrender Prayer

> By means of all created things, without exception,
> the divine assails us, penetrates and moulds us. We
> imagined it as distant and inaccessible, whereas in
> fact we live steeped in its burning layers.
>
> —Pierre Teilhard de Chardin

It takes only one Jacob-like experience to switch the polarities of your world. When you have suffered some angelic defeat that hurls your soul into victory laps, you will find yourself asking a quite sensible question: *How can I get in line for more of these incredible defeats?*

To ask this question is to pray.

This may not sound much like any prayer you know, but as soon as you discover that true human life begins when the little self ends, you will seek some way to keep ending your self. That desire is the seed of prayer.

After carrying on drunkenly at some dinner party—the story goes—Dylan Thomas stood up and lurched for the door, muttering, "Someone's boring me. I think it's me."[1] In seeking to transcend himself with alcohol, Dylan Thomas was surely not alone. More than anything, we want to be free of that "boring me." Hence the alcohol and drugs, reckless sex, extreme sports, binges of shopping or eating or exercising, by which we seek to escape the self, only to become its captive.

For those who seek a way of life characterized by little, often quiet, daily defeats, by which we are freed from the tyranny of the little self and delivered into the realm of the great Self, prayer is the answer.

On Easter night one spring, Pam and I boarded a plane and flew to Charleston, South Carolina. It was dark when we arrived, but this far south the April breeze was warm and fragrant as we walked out of the airport, into a rental car, off to Kiawah Island.

I slept hard that night. The spiritual highs of Holy Week and Easter had been profound, but the physical rigors of twelve services in four days had drained me. The sun was burning the drapes off the windows when I awoke Easter Monday morning. I walked out on the balcony, four floors up, and looked over the ocean to the horizon. It was as if the dark curve of the earth had been cut into the white sky with an X-acto knife. Intimations, I thought, of eternity.

I put on my shorts *(in April!)* and went for my morning run.

At low tide the beach must be a half-mile wide, the sand compact and hard, perfect for biking and running. It is early. A woman walks by picking shells, but after that the closest people are the size of toothpicks in the distance. The wind! It barrels down the wide-open stretches, and I decide to run into it—wiser, it seems, to ride it home.

Ragged clouds scuttle across the water, then the sun breaks through and it feels good. The cool spring air goose fleshes my legs, and in such a gale I might be a cartoon figure, pumping my legs but suspended in stasis.

I raise my face to the sun and let the wind pummel me. After a week of bodily stress this is a rough full-body massage. As I run, I close my eyes. The sun that set the curtains alight burns through my eyelids, and I keep them closed for a moment. It is bright—even with my eyes closed. I have the blessing of light without the distraction of vision. I feel weightless.

I open my eyes and return to earth, but I want to go back.

I know the beach is wide. The nearest soul is still a toothpick. I do not need to see—there is nothing to run into! Hearing the surf to my left, I can navigate by sound. I close my eyes and leave them closed. *One, two, three, four, five, six, seven.* Half panicky, I open them. The scene has not changed; I am running on infinite sand. I drop the curtain again, this time for ten seconds. *Open.* I am a little closer to the water, and one of the toothpicks is now wearing a blue hat, but otherwise, nothing.

I am onto something. I close my eyes now and just run—for twenty seconds this time, and I am only half-worried that I will hit something. Then thirty seconds. Forty-five. Finally I am free. I don't need to count, don't need to see. The wind is howling white in my ears, the surf foaming. I am drinking in the sunlight, gulping down lungfuls of warm sea air.

Seeing nothing, I have no sense of movement, nothing looms and recedes. All the wind rush becomes silence, and I am running into an eternal landscape: a sky that does not end, a sea that stretches to the horizon, and a vast plain of white sand. Sightless, I momentarily lose that thin but merciless boundary between myself and everything else. My ego, for whom running blind is frightfully crazy, loses control of me and I soar. When I open my eyes and stop, panting in weird ex-hilaration, I know that I have been somewhere else and come back. It may have been only for a second or two, but in that place where time leaves off, it doesn't matter. It might as well be forever. I have run out of myself.

Prayer is the gracious gift of God, by means of which we are freed from ourselves and united with all that is divine. Yet that is not likely the first thing that pops to mind when someone mentions prayer. We all begin with the old, conventional caricature. Prayer is a lot of words; it's a dogged attempt to get God's ear, change God's mind, fill the order, get our needs met.

Prayer, says the Westminster Catechism, is "offering our desires to God in the name of Christ for things that agree with His will."[2] There's nothing wrong with that definition, but conventional faith always makes God into the superparent (which is how children first imagine God). Then, as we learned to do with Mom and Dad, our task is to tell God what we want and try, at least, to get our wants to agree with the divine will (which can be tough). If God is the grand authority figure, it seems right for prayer to be, as the Baltimore Catechism has it, the "lifting up of our minds and hearts to God, to adore Him, to thank Him for His benefits, to ask His forgiveness, and to beg of Him all the graces we need whether for soul or body."[3] If God is up there and we are down here and the task is somehow to get what we truly need for our lives without offending him, then this is what prayer should be. It fits very well with the conventional mindset, in which authority is externalized in a reward-and-punishment system.

Prayer always begins in this mode (sadly, for many, it stays here), but like every other component of our spiritual lives, it is meant to crash and burn. We are meant—like Job, like Paul, like Jesus in fact—to pray earnestly, to seek valiantly for things agreeable to God's will, and still to have our prayers go unheard, unanswered, banging hard against the leaden firmament and falling back upon our heads. This is the only way our willfulness comes to an end, the only way we finally acknowledge that, for all our murmuring "thy will be done," our prayer has mostly been an antsy attempt to control situations, people, and outcomes that worry or frighten us. That is normal and natural. All growth in prayer begins in unanswered prayer. It is the failure of our willful prayer that drags us mercifully into a state of willingness.

In Jewish, Christian, and Islamic scriptures we are commanded to pray—passionately, persistently—for our own needs and those of others. In the hands of the little self, however, this prayer inevitably becomes an anxious exercise of control. We all go there. What I am holding out for you now is a passage through that old model and into a new understanding. One where Dylan Thomas's "boring me" is transcended for a moment, just long enough for the great I AM to pray in you.

By now you could predict this paradox, but I will tell you again anyway. True prayer is something you must do, and yet it is not you who does it. Prayer cannot happen unless you will it—set aside the time, sit down in a certain chair—but this is only unlocking the door, putting out the Please Disturb sign, and waiting.

The disciple asks the master, "What can I do to attain God?"

The master answers by asking, "What can you do to make the sun rise?"

The disciple says indignantly, "Then why are you giving us all these methods of prayer?"

And the master replies, "To make sure you're awake when the sun rises."[4]

Prayer, then, is staying awake and aware so that the sunrise can find you. The only *you* that can do such a thing, however, is the God-Self within. And for that to happen, you have to lose that little self.

In speaking of his conversion moment, Dag Hammarskjöld could just as well be describing true prayer:

I don't know Who, or what, put the question, I don't know when it was put. I don't even remember answering. But at

some moment I did answer Yes to Someone, or Something,
and from that hour I was certain that existence is meaningful
and that, therefore, my life, in self-surrender, had a goal.[5]

In one way or another we all seek the thrilling moment of saying
"Yes to Someone, or Something" and knowing that our lives have
meaning and purpose. But the key to that ecstatic glory is this: "my
life, in self-surrender."

We enter the latter stages of prayer when we can begin to let go.
Now prayer morphs from a lot of asking into a way of being. What we
seek is no thing at all, but rather an experience of self-surrender so that
union with God can follow. My blind running on the beaches of
Kiawah was a physical experience of this self-losing.

If we had tried to speak of prayer in this way before you became
aware of your true and false selves, before you had any inkling of the
eternal *now,* there would have been no basis for understanding. That
is why the passage to prayer comes here, in Unconditional Surrender.
*Because if you are to surrender yourself, you must have confident faith in
the One to whom you are surrendering.*

In the early stages of life, you and I are too fearful to surrender.
All we know, really, is the egoic self. God is still the distant Wizard.
Life is rigged against us, and we have to claw for everything good we
get. We're living in hope of reward, in fear of punishment. Who in her
right mind would surrender to a "God" like that, who governed a
world like that?

As you celebrate what Jean-Pierre de Caussade calls "the sacrament of the present moment,"[6] however, and know the basic goodness
of God's whole created order, you start to see surrender differently.
When you come to know the God who meets you in the bedchamber
of your very heart, you are more likely to give in. And once you have
surrendered yourself and found the loss to be a delight (in this way

prayer is, as Song of Songs depicts it immortally, like love-making), you become eager for more such losses.

So what is this prayer that culminates in union with God? It's clearly not the wordy kind, though giving voice to our prayers is essential to both personal and corporate worship. It is not a mechanism for getting what we need, but a trusting relationship. It is not so much communication with God as it is communion with God. The early church fathers spoke often of "becoming prayer." If, as Paul Tillich has expressed it, God is not a being, but Being itself,[7] then prayer becomes simply a resting in that Being. This kind of praying is known as contemplative prayer.

When I describe contemplative prayer, however, you may not recognize it as prayer. That is only because this ancient form of communing with God has fallen into centuries-long disuse. Now it is making a resurgence, in part because the mechanical model of prayer holds so little attraction even for religious people, to say nothing of the nonreligious who still sense a longing for some kind of divine communion. Contemplative prayer has no words, not even any thoughts. It is rooted in interior silence. It is a complete surrender of our whole being to God—not the Wizard in the sky, but God as the ground of our being, the Source from whom our life emerges at every moment. This God is beyond words, beyond our highest thoughts and deepest emotions.

There are many expressions of contemplative prayer, but I can speak only of the one I know. Centering Prayer (one form of contemplative prayer) comes out of the ancient Christian contemplative tradition, notably the Desert Fathers and Mothers, St. John of the Cross, St. Teresa of Avila, and the anonymous, fourteenth-century treatise on prayer that left my chin on my chest, *The Cloud of Unknowing*. It was distilled into a simple method for contemporary seekers in the 1970s by three Trappist monks, one of whom, Abbot Thomas Keating, wrote a best-selling guide to centering prayer, *Open Mind, Open Heart*.

Since I am a minister, you could say I am a professional pray-er. But after years of leading congregations in corporate prayer, and decades of offering my own private prayers according to the forms of the Book of Common Prayer that included petitions for my own needs and those of others, I gave up praying. At least privately. I continued to lead corporate prayer on Sunday mornings, but I had no desire to pray on my own. I had done it religiously for fifteen years, and I was done with it. It was wooden, rote, empty. It should not surprise you that I was forty-five. I know now that as the old "God" was failing me, as the conventional spiritual program of achievement and performance was failing me, the old engine of prayer was going *pocketa-pocketa-plop*.

After an arid season of prayerlessness, I found myself at a clergy conference led by one of those three Trappist monks who helped revive Centering Prayer, Father Basil Pennington. Like all speakers at our annual conferences, Father Pennington gave a brief presentation. But then he sat down on the dais and invited us to sit quietly and open our awareness to God. He taught us to choose a sacred word that symbolized our intention to consent to the presence and action of God in our lives.

I remember the word I chose. I was so tired, I chose *rest*. All I had to do, Father Pennington was saying, as I sat quietly with eyes closed, was silently to offer that word, *rest*. Period. I didn't have to do anything else. I was there simply to open myself to the presence of God.

Of course, my cuticle-nibbling self did not like this, wigged out at the silence, and threw up a hundred critical concerns that needed addressing right now. Nevertheless, blessed Basil's calm voice was assuring me that if thoughts and distractions arose, all that was needed was a silent interposing of my sacred word. *Rest*. When the exercise was over, I felt strangely alive. I went home, found a quiet chair in my bedroom, and sat for twenty minutes doing the unthinkable: nothing. It was as if I had tasted a secret delectation. For the first time in my life I sought prayer not out of some holy obligation but because I loved it. Dare I say it—it was actually pleasurable!

I don't think you can understand contemplative prayer until you have flunked out of the old school of prayer. You can't give yourself to this practice until you have done the inner work of the five passages that have led us to this radical surrender. Because you can't surrender to a God you don't really trust. But once you know the God who does not judge you for love's sake, once you befriend the present moment and know it to be good as is, you are ready to surrender yourself to God, to *now*.

If the essence of all spiritual life is this letting go, contemplative prayer is the sine qua non, the one needful thing. Because, put simply, if you are to let go, you need practice.

All day long you are presented with things that slightly annoy you or that actually cause suffering—a selfish coworker who takes credit for your work, a demanding child, a stalled career, a disease that cannot be cured. To live in joy and peace you must be able to release these things, drop the illusion of control, surrender to this moment, and find that it's all right. But...that is like saying you must run a 26.2-mile marathon before you have jogged a single block.

To be able to let go of the big things in life, you first have to practice letting go of the little things. This is all you are doing when you sit down to pray. For a few minutes you sit quietly and consent to God's presence. God is already present, of course, but will you allow that Presence? Your false self will not easily loosen its grip. There will be an endless string of thoughts, images, feelings. Your only task is to let them go. You do not fight them or judge them (which is only to empower them); you simply let them go with a sacred word. In that moment you are free to sink into the divine Presence. Of course, in the very next moment a thought will drift into your mind, and—once more—you will release it.

A discouraged nun once complained to Thomas Keating, "Oh, Father Thomas, I'm such a failure at this prayer. In twenty minutes I've had ten thousand thoughts."

"How lovely!" said the abbot. "Ten thousand opportunities to return to God!"[8]

Somewhere deep in your heart is a release mechanism for un-hooking all the worries and anxieties that you cannot fix or manage or control. There is a little letting-go muscle that activates that release mechanism, but in most of us that muscle is limp and flaccid from disuse. In contrast, the holding-on muscle is incredibly powerful be-cause we exercise it so continuously and rigorously.[9] Contemplative prayer strengthens the heart's letting-go muscle so that, when we need to release the little naggings and the huge burdens of daily life, we can do it—because we've been practicing. I often think of my prayer time as spiritual calisthenics: strengthening my heart muscle, the one that lets go.

Now this is the only kind of prayer I can give myself to. I still have a list of people I pray for, but I offer these intercessions and pray for my own needs after I have been quiet in the Presence. And often I feel that, wordlessly, I have already laid those burdens in God's lap, and I can simply trust without saying any further prayers.

I do not mean that Centering Prayer is the only method for let-ting go. Brother Lawrence, the one famous for *The Practice of the Presence of God,* confessed that all methods of prayer and meditation discouraged him. He ultimately fell back upon his own simple plan:

to practice the presence of God in the smallest acts of life. To wash the pots and pans as prayer, to do everything as an act of worship—even picking up a straw from the floor.[10]

A woman once came to Archbishop Anthony Bloom, confessing that she had been working at prayer with no sense of God's presence at all. Wisely, the archbishop told her to go back to her home and for fifteen minutes each day to knit before the presence of God. He forbade her to speak of prayer, but only to knit and enjoy the peace of her little room. In time the woman came to discover the Presence that was already and always there. Her knitting itself became a form of contemplation.[11]

My daughter Sharon, who bakes bread every week, once told me, almost up to her elbows in dough, "Kneading bread is better than meditation."

Somehow, though, you must be still, even if you are engaged in walking meditation. Somehow you must shut down your mind, give your tight-fisted will a ten-minute pink slip. Then the wonders start happening. You have at least a moment in the day when you aren't having to be the star of your own show or the butt of your own criticism. An empty space in which you are not judging and evaluating everything but simply letting all those things be. You have a moment when you let God be God, and you are free to be the broken and beautiful child of heaven that you are, the one whom God adores.

I still get giddy when I think of it—how my little needy self could never pray like this! That *me* is too insecure to look at myself as I am, too fearful to see life as the drama in which I will always meet the living God. Yet the miracle that still makes me laugh is that the Spirit of God prays in and through my great Self. There is one Presence before whom I do not have to put on a mask. This is the Presence that envelops the whole of reality, not just the good parts I want to cling to. In its shadow I know that "all things work together for good," as St. Paul says—*all* things.[12] Through every encounter and circumstance, both happy and painful, God is ever coaxing me one step closer to the fire of love.

This sublime prayer of Teilhard de Chardin I hope one day to make my own.

> After having perceived you as he who is "a greater myself," grant, when my hour comes, that I may recognize you under the species of each alien or hostile force that seems bent on destroying or uprooting me. When the signs of age begin to mark my body (and still more when they touch my mind); when the ill that is to diminish or carry me off strikes from without or is born within me; when the painful moment comes in which I suddenly awaken to the fact that I am ill or growing old; and above all at that last moment when I feel I am losing hold of myself and am absolutely passive within the hands of the great unknown energies that have formed me; in all those dark moments, O God, grant that I may understand that it is you (provided only my faith is strong enough) who are painfully parting the fibers of my being to penetrate to the very marrow of my substance and bear me away within yourself.[13]

SEVENTEEN

Seventy Times Seven
Equals One

> Not forgiving is like drinking rat poison and waiting
> for the rat to die.
>
> —Anne Lamott

Mom is not ready to meet her Maker" is the way her son put it. He
was calling to request a pastoral visit. His mother was anxious,
restless, needing to talk to a priest. I had first visited Laura in the hospital when she received her sudden diagnosis. A brain tumor too far
gone. She had a few months to live. They got her stable enough to go
home with hospice, and since she was divorced and lived alone, her
son had taken a leave of absence from work to care for her. I came by
almost every week to sit by her bed and talk. Laura was a stolid prag-
matist, so our conversations were mostly about the technical aspects of
dying: updating the will, seeing to the children, deciding between a
coffin or cremation. Now, apparently, she was ready to talk about
some deeper concerns.

"I have some work to do," Laura said, as I took my usual seat by
her hospital bed set up in the living room. Bach was playing on the old
boom box in the windowsill. "Do you have anything I can read?" I
asked if she might like a book of prayers. No, thank you, she would
like something "more interesting." I said I was sure I could find just

the right book. I asked what she was feeling right now, and after a long pause Laura said, "I'm not ready to die."

I looked into her face and nodded a silent yes. I said nothing but left an open space for her to speak when she was ready.

After a long pause, Laura said, "Have you ever visited people in prison—people who were *sinnuhs*?' She accentuated the word, mimicking the voice of a firebrand southern evangelist. I said that I had visited people in prison, and since we were all sinners—yes, I had.

It was an awkward way to bring up sin, so I simply asked her, "What are you thinking about sin?"

Laura said, "I have some."

"What?" I asked.

"I made a conscious decision not to forgive the Hussy." The "Hussy" was Jackie, the woman with whom her husband had had an affair and then married. I knew the story from years ago. Even now she could not say Jackie's name. "I forgave Mark, but I decided I could never forgive—the Hussy. So…what happens to me if I don't?"

"Why did you forgive Mark?" I asked.

"Because we had that time together at Kate's [their daughter's] graduation from med school, and it was all right. We went for a walk in Chicago that day, and he told me that if he'd known then what would have happened to the family he never would have left me, but there was no way back now, twenty years on."

"You forgave him," I said, "because you loved him?"

"Yes."

"How did that feel?"

"Good. It felt good."

"Then," I said, "don't you want to feel good again?"

"Well…"

After a long silence I said, "All you have to do is forgive Jackie."

She looked at the ceiling and said, "Then I've got a problem."

"Why?"

"Because that's something I can't do."

She turned over on her side and looked at me through the prison-like bars of the hospital bed. "My father cheated on my mother," she whispered, "and that destroyed my family."

"Did you forgive your father?" I asked.

"Yes."

"Why did you forgive him?"

"In my childhood—I adored my father. So I forgave him."

"You forgave him so you could still love him?"

"Yes."

The next time I saw Laura (it is so often this way), she was weaving in and out of consciousness. We could not speak again. I buried Laura four days later, still wondering as I carried her cremains to the altar whether in the twilight of morphine one night a prayer had formed in Laura's mind and these ashes were finally shriven.

This is the culmination of Unconditional Surrender, the ultimate letting go: forgiveness. But what must be released at the outset is everything you think you know about forgiveness.

Laura's story is key to that new understanding. If we were trying to be kind, we would say it illustrates the tragedy of unforgiveness. But if we are free to name it plainly, we would say it illustrates the stupidity of unforgiveness. How else can we describe this refusal to do something that, according to Laura herself, "feels good," that blesses and heals the forgiver? Why would anyone deliberately wound herself?

The answer is, unfortunately, that we are often perversely willing to suffer rather than to let go of all the pet illusions of the little self.

Laura refused to forgive Jackie, even on her deathbed, because the act would have demanded that Laura let go of something that was more precious than the feeling of solace and peace that could have been hers, more precious even than the hope of dying free from this terrible sin she harbored in her heart. What was more important than all of that? What was so precious? Just this: her little righteous self—and the whole world it created, maintained, and enforced.

To forgive Jackie would be to admit that Laura was no better—and maybe sadder and more vicious—than the Hussy. It would mean that Laura wasn't a paragon of righteousness after all. That twenty years of huffing and puffing in front of her children, vilifying *"her,"* was misguided and wrong. It would mean that she had wasted twenty years, had played the fool.

(If you don't see yourself reflected in Laura, please read the story again. Only when you admit your own unforgiveness will you receive the ultimate absolution and then be able to offer it to others.)

To forgive is to let go of our cherished version of reality, the one where we have a starring role, and where law and order reign. *(By God, wrong is wrong and right is right.)* Forgiveness, at its heart, then, is not about replacing bad feelings toward the perpetrator with good feelings. After all the discoveries you have made so far, you will not be surprised to learn that forgiveness is about healing what is wrong with *you.* It is about getting a mind transplant and living, finally, in reality. If that sounds radical or just confusing, please stay with me.

There are thousands of books on forgiveness (because we are all Laura), and many are practical guides: How do I forgive someone who is ignorant or defiant? How can I forgive something so deeply wrong? What do I do when the old feelings of bitterness and anger come back even after I've forgiven someone?

These are important approaches to forgiveness. But, good and important as they are, these therapeutic interventions cannot transform us and break us free—into reality. They are only early-stage, provisional steps that lead us ultimately into the foyer, knocking on the door of the Kingdom.

Are we prepared, finally, to stop tinkering with this little wrong, that enormous crime, this discrete outrage, and lay down the whole hopelessly self-referential make-believe version of reality that we've been living in for forty, fifty, or sixty years?

This is the huge question pulsing through Jesus's parable of the unforgiving servant in Matthew chapter 18. Peter comes to Jesus asking, "Lord, how many times shall I forgive my brother or sister who sins against me? Up to seven times?"[1]

That, apparently, was the standard religious formula of the day. You're required to forgive someone a full seven times, and then you're free to hate on them again. You've earned the right. It's conventional ethics, perfect for little Boy Scouts and Girl Scouts in the morning of life. Perfect for people like us who need some authority figure—the church, the Bible, the Book of Order—to give us the rules that determine who's achieved righteousness and who hasn't. How we love the tit-for-tat system!

Jesus responds with an equation. "I do not say to you, up to seven times, but up to seventy times seven."[2]

We're often told that this is not a literal number—490—but a metaphor of persistence. There ought to be no limit to our forgiveness. Just keep on forgiving endlessly.

Jesus must have judged from the look on Peter's face that he and the others were headed down this very path ("I just have to be a better, stronger, more persistent Boy Scout"), because he quickly tells a game-changing story.

A king calls his servants to settle up accounts. A man is brought before him who owes ten thousand bags of gold, and since he can't repay the debt, the king orders that the man, along with his wife and children and all that he has, be sold to pay at least pennies on the dollar. In utter desperation the servant begs the king, "Be patient with me, and I will pay back everything." So the king has mercy on him, cancels the whole debt, and sets him free.

The servant walks out of the king's chambers and immediately spies a man who owes him a hundred silver coins. He grabs the poor debtor by the throat, throttles him and says, "Pay what you owe me!" This man too pleads for mercy but is denied. He is thrown into debtor's prison until he pays the last coin.

The other servants see this travesty and report the wicked servant to the king, who says, "I forgave you ten thousand bags of gold, and you would not forgive a hundred silver coins?" He throws him into prison.[3]

This is a story of numbers. And the key numbers are ten thousand bags of gold (let's call it ten million dollars) and a hundred silver coins (call it a hundred bucks).

Like all Jesus's parables, this one doesn't pretend to verisimilitude. If you ask how a day-laboring servant could be into his boss for ten million, you miss the point. All we're supposed to understand is: this is a huge, epic debt, and *it is unpayable*. (If ten million is a number you could maybe whittle down if you had twenty or thirty years, then make it a cool billion. Got it? Unpayable.)

Now that we know the astronomical scale of the numbers, we can revisit the servant's response. He's called in, told to pay up his ten million, and what does he say? "Give me a few days to raise the capital." That's like my being presented with the bill for our national debt and saying, "Wow—okay, give me a few days to call some of my buddies. I'll see what I can do." It's crazy. Addicts talk like this when they need just one more fix.

Do you see? It's the sole point of Jesus's parable: when presented with a wildly unpayable debt, the servant insists on paying his way out of it. In Bill W.'s club they call this "stinking thinking."

This is not so much the parable of the unforgiving servant as it is the parable of the *unpayable debt*. It is meant to sweep away our cherished version of reality, the tit-for-tat system where you pay your own way, earn whatever you get in life, and build your own tower of righteousness. It is meant to knock the props out from under our fierce self-sufficiency and drive us into the arms of mercy. But this servant is, like all of us, too stubborn for that. He is not about to be broken by the ten million, not about to be broken even by the grace that forgives him everything. He refuses to live in a world of grace at all. That's for weaklings and losers. That is why he walks out of the presence of mercies by the million and essentially kills a man for a hundred bucks. (It is also the reason why, I think, in the end the king throws him in prison: he hasn't hit bottom yet.)

The point of this parable is not that we should just keep at it, or—even loftier—that we, having been forgiven our millions, should surely forgive the other's hundred bucks. Peter presents forgiveness as a transaction, and Jesus bumps it immediately up to the level of transformation.

That is the riddle of "seventy times seven." What's called for is not a dutiful forgiving that leaves the whole pay-your-way system in place, but a mind transplant, a passing from darkness to light. Once you get that it's all mercy all the time, your egoic sense of right and entitlement begins to melt away. You don't deserve anything. Not because you are a worm, but because you already have everything—and it's all an amazing gift. You didn't create it, you don't own it, and you don't need to cling to it. That's what it means to live in the world of grace, where you have a right to nothing and yet possess everything.

But there is a huge barrier to living in that alternate world. It's the world of juvenile justice. Once you've lived a few decades in that world where good, honest, hard-working people get rewarded and all the rest get the little or nothing they've earned, it's nearly impossible to give it up. Your whole false self is built on it. It's important that you see yourself as good and worthy, in deep contrast to those other people. When someone suggests that no one is any better or worse than anyone else, or that no one has a right to anything he has, it's an outrage. You've been playing by the rules all your life, and—more often than not—you've been a winner.

So when someone comes along saying there really are no winners and losers, it's a slap in the face. And not just in your face—in God's. *He* made it very clear that sinners will be punished and the righteous rewarded. You've worked hard all your life to be as righteous as you could. Of course nobody's perfect, but what grinds your gears is the people who don't even *try*!

Letting go of this system of justice so that we can live in the kingdom of mercy is the totality of Jesus's teaching on forgiveness.

The Greek *aphieme* is translated "to forgive," but it means "to release from one's grasp," "to let go," "to set free." To forgive is to let go of the world of just deserts. Give it up. Change your entire outlook.

This is the wisdom of Jesus's equation. "Not seven times, but seventy times seven." It's a koan. I believe the equation is $70 \times 7 = 1$. *There is only one act of forgiveness.* It's reserved for grownups.

Here's what I mean: After you've lived in that cherished world of just deserts and it fails you—you don't get what a good person like you really deserves (while other, lesser people prosper), and you're angry, bitter—you are called upon to forgive it all. The whole thing. Forgive God for being such a whopping disappointment. Forgive people for being so fickle, mean, and selfish (along with all the things you love about them). Forgive the world for being so unfair and yet so beautiful. And finally, the pardon that galls us all: forgive yourself for being, well, like everybody else: fickle, mean, and selfish (along with all the things you love about yourself).

Seventy-times-seven-equals-one is a single letting go of your completely mistaken view of life, God, people, the universe. Do not waste any more time, Jesus means, toting up discrete acts of forgiveness that are founded on a lie. It is as if you are standing within your egoic kingdom, its imaginary boundaries clearly marked, and someone steps over the line, trespasses, offends you. And you forgive them. But such offenses are not real. They exist only in the ego's made-up world.

It's not right that your brother stole your share of the inheritance when Dad died. Worse, he won't even admit it. It's unforgivable! Unless you no longer believe you have a right to any share—in anything —and that any share you happen to receive is a gift.

I spread lies about you and ruin your reputation. You've either got to sue me or forgive me. But, Jesus wonders, what if? What if you didn't really care about your reputation? What if you were so certain of your true identity, the deep *I* that cannot be touched by any calumny, that you just let the offense go? Like a mother whose exhausted and frustrated child is pounding his little fists into her knees. Does she respond as if she's being attacked? She disarms the child by enfolding him in her embrace.

There's a story that says this perfectly. It's a beloved anecdote from the Desert Fathers, those third- and fourth-century hermits who slipped off into the Egyptian desert to be visited by solitude and enriched by nothingness.

> Two old men had lived together for many years and they had never fought with one another. The first said to the other, "Let us also have a fight like other men." The other replied, "I do not know how to fight." The first said to him, "Look, I will put a brick between us and I will say, 'It is mine,' and you will reply, 'No, it is mine,' and so the fight will begin." So they put a brick between them and the first said, "This brick is mine," and the other said, "No, it is mine." And the first replied, "If it is yours, take it and go." So they gave it up without being able to find a cause for an argument.[4]

Imagine living like that, Jesus says. It's actually possible to live in a world where you don't need to forgive all those offenses—because you just don't take offense anymore. And it's possible once you grant the one great big universal forgiveness: 70 x 7 = 1.

Most of us are struggling to forgive all the usual crimes against humanity. Children have spurned our love. Friends have betrayed us. Bosses have thrown us under the bus. Husbands and wives have hurt us deeply. We keep living in that unreal world where we expect people to be better than they are: sinful, broken. And when they prove only human, we act dumbfounded. We keep living as if we ourselves were somehow one rung above others on the ladder of humanity, and we are wounded and hurt when they can't join us at this higher level. As a result, there are endless offenses.

It's pure delusion. You can follow a four-step forgiveness process to lessen your suffering and restore justice and order in that make-believe world, but once you've been through this cycle a few hundred times, isn't it time you let all that go? Radical forgiveness is not interested in helping you forgive a thousand hurts. It seeks instead to save you from suffering a thousand hurts in the first place.

Yes, there will always be hurts; they come as the cost of living. But you don't need to create more hurts yourself. As the Buddhist saying goes, "Pain is inevitable, suffering is optional." Most of the suffering we endure is self-caused, the result of living in that world of juvenile justice. When we recognize this, we let that suffering go. Release it. We're human so it's never final. Some perceived offense wounds us, and we have to let it go again. By forgiveness, we choose—right now—to live in the kingdom of mercy. "Forgiveness is not an occasional art," said Martin Luther, "it is a permanent attitude."[5]

To understand forgiveness as releasing your own illusions is not easy. It will not make sense in the "real world." Don't tell your friends about this new notion of forgiveness you've read about. (They will think you're eating strange mushrooms.) Just live inside it for a while. See how much suffering you avoid by living inside the truth: about life, about others, about yourself.

Suddenly you will understand things that were once maddening. How could Jesus possibly say, "Happy are you when people insult you and persecute you, and say untrue things about you"? Any normal person would take offense! Surely he can't mean it when he says, "If someone hits you on the right cheek, give him your left as well." And we can hardly forgive him for saying something so plainly idiotic as "Love your enemies." You will always go crazy trying to see deep wisdom when you are surrounded by Funhouse mirrors. But step inside the Kingdom. Once your consciousness has been altered, what seemed crazy appears natural.[6]

The "normal" world finds it oddly wonderful when the Amish forgive a man who walks into a school and guns down ten little girls, killing five. We read the story, pause in amazement, then turn the page. *Maybe in their strange world....* We hear staggering stories of forgiveness from black South Africans in the Truth and Reconciliation movement. It's inspiring, but it wouldn't work where we live, in the sensible world of lethal-injection justice. But these radical forgivers have all decided not to be dragged into the demented world of the savage and violent. They have forgiven in order to save their sanity, to stay in the light, to live in the truth.

Finally you will begin to understand the forgiveness of God. Now when you sing "Amazing Grace," you will understand what's so amazing. Not that God is so big he manages to keep up with a planet full of wretches, forgiving a billion sins a second, but that God has taken one look at this fearful and sublime world, one look at us humans in all our shame and glory, one look at the whole Big Banging creation, and decided not to take offense. God forgives, but only once, a blanket pardon that covers every sin past, present, and to come. Forever.

And so, Jesus says, should you.

Everything Belongs

> And the stars down so close, and sadness and pleasure
> so close together, really the same thing.... The stars
> are close and dear and I have joined the brotherhood
> of the worlds. And everything's holy—everything,
> even me.
>
> —John Steinbeck, *The Grapes of Wrath*

> Thanks, thanks for everything, praise, praise for it all.
>
> —St. John Chrysostom's farewell

The path of Unconditional Surrender is like a funnel. It starts out small and gets wider and wider. It begins in a dim awareness that a shift is on and that things are being pulled away ("Tidal Turn"), and with a little grace we learn to release larger and larger clutches ("The Surrender Prayer").

If you have ever hated the notion of cleaning out a bloated closet or a cluttered garage—but found that once you start ditching crap it feels so good you almost can't stop—you know how this works. Eventually we realize that what cries out for release are not a lot of little things but the one big thing: our little-mind consciousness. For the closet and garage cleaner, it means you start asking, *How come we live in this big chaos-creating house in the first place?* Spiritually, it means you dare to ask, *What makes me think I deserve this, have earned that? What makes me imagine I'm better than anyone else, or that people should be anything other than the lovely messes they so obviously are?* Forgiveness begins (70 x 7 = 1).

When you get to this point, you spend less and less time trying to decide whether to let go of this or that or the other. All that sorting presumes you know what to keep and what to unhand, what's good or bad, valuable or detrimental. In a word, you waive your right to be the judge of everything.

Jesus said what all the sages have said, "Judge not." Yet early-stage faith is mostly judgmental. It has to divide everything into two neat piles:

- This is right; that is terribly, obviously wrong.
- This is good; that is bad, scary, and dangerous.

As you could guess by now, the little self is the one with the august robes and banging gavel who hands down all these binary judgments. True to its nature, what is pronounced good are all the things that fit nicely inside its comfortable worldview, all the things that make it look fabulous, all the people who are agreeable and supportive. All the rest is bad.

This black-and-white system of judging is called dualism. In the early years it's the only thing we know. We start out learning right from wrong. It's an important step in our moral development, to say nothing of its value in passing true-false quizzes. This simple categorization helps us to identify the geeks and nerds we wish at all costs to avoid and to locate the cool people we hope desperately to join. Healthy adolescents are very opinionated; they tell you what they adore and what they hate.

As we mature into adulthood, however, we're meant to lessen this highly contrasted view of things, learning to appreciate nuance, tolerate contradiction, and recognize our own darkness. But often this polarity hangs on and becomes a long-term way of living.

As we noted in chapter 11, the need to appear good and right leads us to cut off the "bad" parts of ourselves and stuff them down in that cellar—the place where demons are born. The dualistic self maintains a firewall between the light side it presents to the world and the dark side it cannot look on. The light it judges good, and the dark it judges evil. It is harsh on the shadow it sees in others, but it can also be merciless on itself, since self-condemnation so clearly proves that I am a principled and good person.

This is the passage on the journey when we surrender the robes and the gavel, step down from the bench. "Judge not."

We must let go our judging because what we most need at this stage of life is a radical inclusion, an indiscriminate embrace. What the soul seeks in the second age of faith is not rightness anymore but wholeness. For that, the old magistrate in you must be gone; the old dualism has to melt into one.

Remember "It's Not About Being Good Anymore"? You don't need to waste your life figuring if you're worthy or not. You are, even though you are a normal human hobbled by sin. God embraces you completely. God does not judge you. Jesus says so (see John 3:16–17). Therefore do not judge yourself.

When you can embrace your commingled self, you are able to accept others as *they* are. You stop judging people.

Now is the season to open that cellar door and welcome all those shunted off parts of yourself, learn to love them as God loves each of the multiple selves that make up *you*, the honorable ones and the shameful ones too.

Finally, this is the time to retract all those verdicts on your past. For years the judge in you has written with a black Sharpie all over the timeline of your life. This childhood wounding is labeled "Destructive." That early career move is covered in "Mistake." Your divorce is scribbled over with "Not my fault!" The cancer battle is marked with "Why me?" The moment a business partner betrayed you is "Wrong, wrong, wrong." All of these must be erased, removed because they are the scrawlings of the dualistic self, dividing everything into *the things that were good and right and just* and *the things that should never have happened!*

That ruthless division collapses with one experience of injustice, betrayal, or wrong that blossoms into blessing. You are humbled. *Who am I to decide what is good and right for me?*

After I failed the oral exams for my PhD, I lay awake nights cursing my destiny. Only years later could I see that God used my failure to bring about my blessing. I think of all the people I have been privileged to know who have said, "Thank God for my addiction." It was the gateway to grace, mercy, and forgiveness. All it takes is one or two profound moments of awe and wonder, at the way our wrongs turned out beautifully—if painfully—right, and we step down from the bench.

All the great men and women have at least in some way begun this journey into wholeness. They have stopped judging the world and life and people—and just started accepting it all. The mystics call this "detachment." It's simply letting life have its say, letting people be who they are. It's taking tea with your demons, taking a walk with your shadow.

Once you understand God's power to use any and all means to bring us to salvation, you discover that, as Richard Rohr puts it, "Everything belongs."[1] Not just the things you declare good and acceptable, but all the wrongs you have endured, the wrongs you have done—the whole grab bag. In God's economy everything belongs, even and especially our mistakes and failures. In the alchemy of grace, these are the iron God turns to gold.

Carl Jung writes, "God is the name by which I designate all things which cross my path violently and recklessly, all things which alter my plans and intentions, and change the course of my life, for better or for worse."[2]

Only someone who had learned how to trust, how to forgive, only someone who had found blessing in defeat, could say such a thing. But I find many people who have learned to sing this same remarkable song.

Last September I was privileged to officiate at my niece's wedding in Atlanta. We all gathered in the church for the rehearsal, which is when Pam and I met Carie. She was a bridesmaid and needed someone to hold her infant child while she took her place with the bridal party at the altar. Pam immediately offered to hold the little girl with whom she would fall in love. Her name was Trinity.

When Carie placed Trinity in Pam's arms, the baby was like a rag doll, her arms and legs limp, her head bobbling on her neck. She cried, and Pam walked her outside, soothed her until she fell asleep. All weekend Pam had the magic touch with Trinity. She didn't know what disease had weakened this child. It wasn't until later, sitting with Carie, that she learned that Trinity had cerebral palsy. She was Carie and Josh's fourth child. Trinity's older brother Wyatt had Down syndrome.

This was a family I wanted to know.

"For the first five years we couldn't conceive a child," Carie told us, "so we adopted our son Wesley through the foster care system. Then two years later we conceived twins! They told us there was a three percent chance that one of the twins had a chromosomal abnormality. They could have done more tests—but there were risks. And besides, Josh and I knew that this child was already ours.

"We didn't know until the day Wyatt was born that he had Down syndrome, but that wasn't the big deal. I had these twins at thirty-one weeks, and the boys were two and three pounds, so our big concern was just, 'Alive? Breathing?'

"On two different occasions Wyatt almost died. We had to pray for his life. From the very first we had to *want* him. The impulse of your heart tells you what you love before you can really think about it. And now he's the light of our lives. We adore him.

"We always knew we wanted to adopt again, and because of Wyatt, we were open to another child with special needs. When we first visited Trinity, she was about nine months. She wasn't even rolling over, when most kids that age are already sitting up. I was afraid. She wasn't diagnosed yet, but I saw her rigid movements and I feared something terrible. Here we were with three boys already, one with special needs. Should we do this? *Could* we do this? Why did God bring us to this child? We were confused.

"We were in the process with Trinity for a couple months. I had already made up my mind, but I wanted Josh to have space to say yes or no. Then finally he said, 'I can't get her smile out of my head.' And Trinity was our baby.

"She was diagnosed with cerebral palsy the day we took her home. At eleven months, no one could really predict anything. Would she ever walk? No one could say. We're an active family. How will it be if one of us can't walk? But our fears turned to peace. We knew Trinity was our daughter, and it would be all right.

"We have struggles every day. This isn't easy. Somehow we ended up with this crazy unique family! But we wouldn't trade this for something 'normal.' You're so afraid of not being 'normal' or 'perfect' until you live with it for a while, and then it looks the opposite. You realize it's true: the last shall be first."

This woman is, in Robert Frost's words, "one acquainted with the night." She can look into the darkness of doubt, the shadow of death, and literally watch fear turn to peace. That's almost typical in people who have lived with some painful problem that can't be made to go away. The rest of us always have one more trick up our sleeve. But they have to sit in darkness until it becomes that luminous darkness we spoke of. Then they no longer want a perfect child or a perfect life, because they understand that when you live only in the light there is no depth of heart, no wisdom of the soul. Bearing Wyatt, adopting Trinity, Carie knew: everything belongs.

This is the final chapter in this passage, the climax of this long process we began together many pages ago. I want to close with one further aspect of this reality that "everything belongs."

As you seek to grow, to leave earlier stages that you have out-grown—that no longer serve you—it's easy to kick yourself for living so long in that old incarnation. We are very good at judging ourselves. *Why didn't I see this twenty years ago? Think of the messes I could have avoided. Think of what I could have become.* But every phase is impor-tant. You can't skip a stage; there is no fast track to enlightenment.

Erik Erikson, who pioneered the stages of human psychological development, saw the process like an unfolding rosebud. Each petal opens at a certain time, in a certain order. First the outermost petals peel away until gradually the inner flower unfolds. If you interfere with the natural order and try to pull back the innermost petals, you destroy the whole flower.[3]

As you gain wisdom (which is the same as saying: as you endure suffering without fleeing), you come to know that the missteps and failures, the disappointments and heartbreaks—all the things you re-sent in others or regret in yourself—were actually the transformative experiences that drew you to a deeper level. What you discover in the latter stages of faith is that all the earlier stages were absurdly necessary. Especially the moments when you could not, by force of will, make it come out right.

When I look back on my life and replay the scenes of my pathetic immaturity or pitiful failure, I want to delete those files and pretend that those things happened to someone else, a bad prototype of myself that I have now replaced with a new version that looks almost like Mohandas Gandhi. It's just my little *self* going on, of course. Upon entering a new stage in life, the Mini-Me has to destroy all the embarrassing evidence of its past. I'm better than that now, and when I see others who remind me of my previous self, I sniff a lot. I prove how superior I am by rejecting what I now consider inferior. You probably do the same. That's why it's so important to understand: everything belongs.

Thomas Keating writes, "No aspect of human nature or period of human life is to be rejected but integrated into each successive level of unfolding self-consciousness. In this way the partial goodness proper to each stage of human development is preserved and only its limitations are left behind."[4] The goal (which takes a little more grace than I now have) is to look back and love yourself at every stage of your life. No matter how partial the goodness, it is all good and utterly necessary for your salvation.

In his book *Overcoming Life's Disappointments,* Harold Kushner works a wonderful midrash on the story of Moses's breaking the first stone tablets of the Decalogue.[5]

After his transcendent mountaintop rendezvous with Yahweh, Moses descends with the two tablets of stone given him by the Almighty, bearing the divine words "written with the finger of God."[6] There, however, Moses finds the Israelites worshiping a golden calf.

"Moses' anger burned hot," we read, "and he threw the tablets from his hands and broke them at the foot of the mountain."[7]

For Moses, Kushner says, the dream was over. The hope of creating from a slave people a new community who would perfectly follow the commandments of God and live in shalom—it all came to a pathetic end when he saw the Israelites dancing before a bovine idol. His "anger burned hot." He dashed the stone tablets to the ground.

I know what that feels like. To see the dream of perfection not just falter a little but fail pretty ugly. No one could have blamed Moses if he had walked away and given up on God and the people of God—and himself. It's what many, many people do when they are properly disillusioned with God and faith and religion and their worn-out self. But two things happen next that have me slow clapping.

Moses has his meltdown, and then, the Bible says, God summons him back to the mountain peak for the Ten Commandments: Part II. The second version is heartbreakingly human.

"The LORD said to Moses, 'Cut two tablets of stone like the former ones, and I will write on the tablets the words that were on the former tablets, which you broke.'"[8] Cut what? The first time up the mountain God just miraculously presented Moses with the stone tablets. This time Moses has to get his hammer and chisel and get to work.

In this version of faith the heavenly tablets aren't just dropped into your arms. You have to work as a co-creator with God, using the rocks in your backyard and the ordinary tools in your red metal toolbox from The Home Depot. I like this already.

And even though God says, "I will write on the tablets the words that were on the former tablets," he doesn't, exactly. In the end God says, "Write these words.… [Moses] wrote on the tablets the words of the covenant, the ten commandments."[9] In this version of faith you don't get "the finger of God" to do the work for you; instead, you listen for God's voice and start chiseling as fast as you can.

The second thing that happens we know only from the wisdom of the Talmud. Anyone who's read the Bible (or seen *Raiders of the Lost Ark*) knows that the stone tablets of the Ten Commandments were placed inside the ark of the covenant and eventually enshrined in the temple's holy of holies.

But the Talmudic rabbis tell the untold story. After the original tablets were shattered, the people of Israel gathered up the shards and placed them, alongside the whole tablets, in the ark. The broken pieces aren't swept up and gotten rid of. Astonishingly, they hold on to these symbols of their infidelity, their rejection of God, the worst day in their lives—just the kind of thing most of us would want to forget forever. They nestle the shattered dream in with the second version of their lives, so that they will never forget who they are: the very chosen people of God who are also huge, honking sinners. They refuse to lock their shadow in some underground bunker, knowing that whatever they deny will be charged with malignant power. Instead, they place their darkness on display in the holiest place they can think of. Here it rests in the *Shekinah* presence of God, who takes our sin and exchanges it for glory.

Everything belongs.

THE SIXTH PASSAGE

HABITS OF THE HEART

NINETEEN

Do This

> Until you dig a hole, you plant a tree, you water it and make it survive, you haven't done a thing. You are just talking.
>
> —Wangari Muta Maathai, Nobel Laureate

> I like your Christ, I do not like your Christians. Your Christians are so unlike your Christ.
>
> —Mohandas Gandhi

This final passage could as easily be the first. This is where we begin to *do* what we *know*.

You may be wondering how this could as easily go first. *Don't we have to know something before we can do it?* The answer, I'm afraid, is yes and no. Knowledge certainly helps, but spiritual truths only unfurl and reveal their glory when they are enacted. A coach can be immensely helpful in teaching you to swim, but only if you are willing to get in the water. In the same way, we grow spiritually by putting new knowledge into action. We could even say, we know it only by doing it.

What's more, this action we speak of in the spiritual life is almost never a big, heroic deed. It is, instead, a commitment to do very small, seemingly insignificant things day in and day out for years on end.

That's why this last passage is called Habits of the Heart. We are finally changed, transformed by the things we do almost unconsciously, habitually, by heart. In this final passage we move into habits that enable us to live the truths revealed all along the path we've walked since chapter 1—and keep living them one day at a time.

On March 24, 1996, the father of Leon Wieseltier died. Wieseltier was then forty-four years old. As the literary editor of the *New Republic,* he was among the political and literary elite of Washington and New York. Like so many sophisticates, he had left behind the Jewish faith of his youth. Nevertheless, he decided to do what mourning sons are commanded to do.

"In the year that followed, I said the prayer known as the mourner's kaddish three times daily," he writes, "during the morning service, the afternoon service, and the evening service, in a synagogue in Washington and, when I was away from home, in synagogues elsewhere. It was my duty to say it."[1]

I always thought that the Hebrew kaddish must be something like the prayers for the dead in our funeral liturgies. It's not. There are Hebrew prayers for the dead—*yizkor*—but kaddish is a *mitzvah* (commandment) performed on behalf of the departed. It's the mitzvah, found in Leviticus 22:32, to publicly sanctify God's name. Accordingly, kaddish is only about God—God's beauty and majesty. "May his great name be blessed always and forever. Blessed and praised and glorified and exalted and honored and uplifted and lauded be the name of the Holy One." Three times a day, every day, this is what Leon Wieseltier prayed. Whether he felt like it or not. If he was in town or on the road.

Since the whole point of kaddish is to publicly proclaim God's greatness, you can't say kaddish in your own home or in the car while you're driving somewhere. You must find your way to a synagogue service in order to offer your mitzvah in the presence of others who can say "Amen." Even if you're a big-time important person. With a demanding job. With lots of travel. Wieseltier still found his way to a synagogue, somehow, three times a day for a year.

Pretty soon he discovered something happening in his inner life. He was being changed. "It was not long before I understood that I would not succeed in insulating the rest of my existence from the impact of this obscure and arduous practice. The symbols were seeping into everything. A season of sorrow became a season of soul-renovation."[2]

Wieseltier's story points to the two complementary principles at work in the realm of faith: word and action. It is important to know the word, the story, the essential teachings—the Ten Commandments, the Sermon on the Mount, the Five Pillars, the Four Noble Truths. Learning these truths, mastering them, even memorizing them, is always at the heart of faith and is usually the task of our formative years. But every tradition is quite clear that, as important as the word is, if it is to work your transformation, it must be enacted. It is not enough to know the truth; you must put it into practice. To paraphrase Mark Twain, the difference between knowing the truth and doing one little true act is the difference between a lightning bug and lightning. So Leon Wieseltier discovered. He knew all about kaddish, learned it as a boy. What set off within him a "soul-renovation," however, was not only his knowledge of this mitzvah but also his practice of it.

The key here is transformation. Early-stage faith is often taken up with learning the word, mastering the essential stories and precepts. In our early years some of us amassed great knowledge of the Bible, denominational theology, and church history, as well as the unique spirituality of our little group. It afforded us an intuition of the sacred and, at times, a deep sense of identity and belonging within the family and faith community.

But it was, even into our adult years, a child's version. We could tell the stories, recite the words, but when the storms of Act 2 descended on us, that theoretical faith blew away like matchsticks before a twister.

Now if you haven't given up completely on faith, the only kind you have time for is the kind that actually changes your life. It's transformation, or it's nothing at all. The path to transformation, it turns out, runs straight through action. You already know enough *about God,* now it's time for an actual experience *of God.* Time to put knowledge into practice. And the secret that spells the difference between spiritual lightning and mere lightning bugs is no different from the secret of riding a bicycle or learning to swim. You can watch other people do it, you can talk about doing it, you can start out then chicken out, but finally, you have to do it. Pedal till you, falling, fly. Jump in with the fishies.

Action is a kind of everyday miracle. "We become just by the practice of just actions," said Aristotle, "self-controlled by exercising self-control, and courageous by performing acts of courage."[3]

We *do* our way into *being.* Most of us are trying to live that principle in reverse, working harder and harder to *be* better so that we will *do* better. But, as C. S. Lewis observes, it is easier to act our way into feeling than to feel our way into action.[4] Or as the friends of Bill W. put it, "Fake it till you make it." There is great power in simply doing something—whether you believe it or feel it.

I heard a story once of a Marxist intellectual who confessed to a wise Orthodox priest that he could not believe in any of these creeds of the church. The priest was not the least concerned to overcome the man's agnosticism. Instead, he told the man to cross himself and do a hundred solemn prostrations—facedown on the floor—each day in the quiet of his own room. Then come see him if and when he felt like it. Thirty days later the man was back, asking to be baptized.[5]

Especially for people who are trapped in the left hemisphere of their brains (nearly everyone in the modern/postmodern West), this is the wisdom we need to hear. Forget about the twenty things you can't believe, and start doing one true thing, no matter how you feel about it. Bow down with your body, breathe a prayer, touch the sick, feed the hungry, laugh, "consider the lilies." We *do* our way into *being*.

By now you know your way around this central paradox: it is crucial that we step out and act—that we do these things—but our action is only an invitation, an assent to the presence and action of God in our lives. God is the One who works the slow miracle of transformation. All we do is say yes with our lives, with our very bodies.

The problem of knowing the truth but not actually doing it goes back a long ways. As the people of Israel sit in exile, God says to the prophet Ezekiel, "They sit before you as my people, and they hear your words, but they will not obey them. For flattery is on their lips, but their heart is set on their gain."[6] After the Sermon on the Mount, the heart and soul of his teaching, Jesus closes with a call to action.

> Everyone then who hears these words of mine and acts on
> them will be like a wise man who built his house on rock. The
> rain fell, the floods came, and the winds blew and beat on that
> house, but it did not fall, because it had been founded on rock.
> And everyone who hears these words of mine and does not act
> on them will be like a foolish man who built his house on
> sand. The rain fell, and the floods came, and the winds blew
> and beat against that house, and it fell—and great was its fall![7]

The word comes to life only when it is put into practice. That's why the three Abrahamic faiths have all made doing the ground of their being.

The Jews never issued an official creed that must be believed in order to belong to Judaism. Observance—circumcision, Sabbath-keeping, kosher eating—has always been definitive.

In the same way, Islam begins with a statement affirming one God and Muhammad as his prophet. After that, it's all what you do.

Christianity began in the same vein. The earliest believers were known as people of "the Way."[8] They had deeply held beliefs, but what defined them was the way they lived those convictions. In catechesis, the two-year period of preparation for baptism, the new initiates would worship with the Christian community (though they could not yet celebrate the Eucharist). Someone would teach and mentor the catechumens in what Christians thought and how they incorporated their beliefs into their lives and work.

Christianity began with this radical insistence on practicing its beliefs. But as it became more influenced by the Greek penchant for abstract reason, Christianity slowly morphed into a religion emphasizing theology and creed. In the New Testament book of James, we already have a letter of protest against a piety that has forgotten its practice. "Faith without works is dead," it declares.[9]

In emphasizing the interactive balance of word and action, then, we are simply returning to the roots of Judaism, Christianity, and Islam, to say nothing of the Eastern religions that have, since the Axial Age, maintained that their truths can only be fully experienced in the exercise of compassion and justice in daily life.

Once we understand the miracle power of action to break open truth, we need to know one thing more: it happens slowly, quietly, incrementally. In *The Art of Loving,* Erich Fromm writes,

> The practice of any art has certain general requirements, quite
> regardless of whether we deal with the art of carpentry,
> medicine, or the art of love. First of all, the practice of an art

requires *discipline*. I shall never be good at anything if I do not do it in a disciplined way; anything I do if "I am in the mood" may be a nice or amusing hobby, but I shall never become a master in that art.... Without such discipline...life becomes shattered, chaotic, and lacks in concentration.[10]

Most of us think virtues like love and faith belong in a squishier category than carpentry or medicine—but they don't.

I remember reading an article by Atul Gawande, who writes for the *New Yorker* on medicine and health, about how the world's best surgeons got that way. Talent helps. There are a rare few who have the manual dexterity to pick up complex movements before others—even so, that's not what most impresses attending surgeons. They're more interested, Gawande says, in "finding people who are conscientious, industrious, and boneheaded enough to keep practicing this one difficult thing day and night for years on end."[11] You can teach skill, they believe, but not tenacity.

What's true for great surgeons holds across the board. "There have now been many studies of elite performers," Gawande writes, "—concert violinists, chess grand masters, professional ice-skaters, mathematicians, and so forth—and the biggest difference researchers find between them and lesser performers is the amount of deliberate practice they've accumulated. Indeed, the most important talent may be the talent for practice itself."[12] Just so, if you want to change your life, there is no substitute for boneheaded practice.

When Albert Ellis, the iconoclastic psychologist, died in 2007, I read his obituary. Turns out Ellis was a bright but painfully shy young man. At nineteen, however, he set out to change that. He went to a park near his home and staked out a bench, determined to talk to every woman who sat there alone. In one month he spoke to one hundred thirty women.

"Thirty walked away immediately," Ellis recalls. "I talked to the 100, for the first time in my life, no matter how anxious I was. Nobody vomited and ran away. Nobody called the cops."[13]

Though he got only one date as a result of his stakeout, he lost his shyness. Ellis used the same dogged technique to shed his phobia of public speaking, doing it over and over until he became an accomplished speaker.

W. S. Merwin was Poet Laureate of the United States in 2010. But at eighteen he had gone to seek advice from Ezra Pound, the great poet who counseled and blue-penciled the likes of T. S. Eliot. How could he be a great poet? Pound said, "Write 75 lines a day."[14]

You can't be a poet if you don't know your words. But finally you have to scratch those words in some order on the page, punch them letter by letter onto a screen. It doesn't matter if they are any good, which is what the ego wants to kvetch about all day, doing nothing. Just do it.

The path to personal transformation—call it salvation, enlightenment, sanctification—is always a commitment, like that of Albert Ellis, to do something every day. To keep on doing it day after day. In spiritual formation we call it a rule of life or a spiritual practice.

Across all religious traditions there are three classic practices: prayer/meditation, study, and service. It's a daily commitment. It doesn't have to be much; in fact, when you're first getting started, a good spiritual director will make sure that you make it so simple you cannot fail. But whatever it is, it is your rule, your practice.

The beauty is, you don't have to get up each new morning and try to figure out what the path is today. You follow your rule even when it seems not to be getting you anywhere. If you are serious about this journey, you will probably want to find a spiritual director who can help shape the best practice for you and hold you accountable. Should you become restless for something different, the director can help you discern whether the Spirit is leading you in a new direction or whether your ego is getting nervous, wishing to escape the gradual changes overtaking your soul.

This stuff works. Your little *self* doesn't trust it, which is why you must. A friend of mine who's in AA once told me, "The reason people don't use the Twelve Step tools is because they work—and that kind of change scares us." In other words, the ego will suggest you watch *Good Morning America* today rather than sit for prayer because it sees the threatening trajectory of your changing new life, even if you can't.

You can do this. Like me, you are always wishing for some miracle experience that will transform your life in an instant. But this is where we learn the adult lessons of deep, inner transformation and the daily practices that open a space in which God can work.

On January 15, 2009, one hundred fifty passengers aboard US Airways Flight 1549 were gripping their ankles in brace position and praying for their lives. After the plane successfully ditched in the river without losing a single life, their watery ordeal quickly became Miracle on the Hudson. They were all in the maws of death—halfway down the gullet—when they slipped free.

When that happens to you in America, you become a walking miracle. People assume your life will never be quite the same. The rest of us are not really expected to wake up to the evanescent glory of life; we haven't had an as-seen-on-TV miracle happen to us. But surely these people would be forever changed.

A year after the marvel, reporters followed up with the survivors. After their near-death experience, most of the one hundred fifty had made themselves promises. They were going to live differently. They wouldn't spend so much time at the office. They'd go to more hockey games and take more walks with their husbands or wives. They'd stop and tell people just how special they were. A year later some had kept those promises, but most hadn't—or not as well as they intended.[15]

That shouldn't surprise us. Big, sensational events get our attention and sometimes force a quick change in behavior. I knew a man who nearly had a heart attack, had bypass surgery, then lost weight and changed his diet. But only for a while. Then, to the consternation of his wife and friends, he reverted to his old behavior. I've sat with plenty of people who had been given some kind of miraculous reprieve: the deadly test results were mistaken; she walked away from a mangle of car metal with only a broken clavicle; the judge threw out his DUI. Whew! Things will be different now. We're done sleepwalking through life.

Almost always there is an initial change, but just as often it fades. That's because miracles don't change us. Human beings are both awesome and awful creatures of habit. The things we do over and over, day after day, are what shape and form us. Pale, necrotic habits come naturally. If we want to live transformed lives, however, there is one path: a daily spiritual practice. It's all about what we eat and how we exercise our bodies, the rituals that sustain deep personal relationships, and the things that fill our minds. It's a way of life with limits and boundaries. Time for prayer and time for play—crazy, mindless fun. Time for work and time for rest. Time for serving those who need the gifts we have to give.

When it comes to the transformation of life, it doesn't help to walk off a sinking plane unless we walk onto the path that Eugene Peterson calls "a long obedience in the same direction."[16] This, then, is where we stop hoping for the spiritual equivalent of the lottery.

Spiritual practices are something we come back to in the second half of life.

As children we were given a set of practices. I remember mine. On Saturday night I was forced to come in from play and do two things: fill in my Sunday school workbook and polish my shoes. Both good for a boy's soul. I memorized Bible verses, sang gospel songs until I knew the choruses by heart. I went to church every Sunday and to prayer meeting on Wednesday night.

If we're raised in a believing home, we are often habituated in the faith—in beautiful ways. But as we grow older and our minds develop, as we begin to reason and ask *Why?*, the early customs come in for scrutiny. Now we want *to know*. We want proof. We wouldn't be caught dead in anybody's Sunday school class. How harebrained is it to polish your shoes to please the Lord?

We have to leave behind those old patterns of belief. For a time most of us live without any spiritual practices, because the egoic self is naturally on the rise, and it has no time for silly things like pinning a perfect Sunday school attendance medal to your dress. It imagines that now everything good and true can be known in the mind. The stories, customs, and odd little rituals of faith are, by the almighty intellect, ruled out of order. What faith remains is cleansed of all such petty devotions and enshrined as metaphysical principles in the mind.

Some people live like that until they die. The rest of us would have stayed there in the cool heights of the mind, except we couldn't. Some loss, some ordinary suffering, broke us down and our oversized brains collapsed under their own weight. We couldn't think our way back to life; we couldn't reason our way to happiness. There was no explaining it, but praying brought hope. Walking or knitting or painting or writing—done with intention—made the dark clouds lift. Reading the gospel of John again was like hearing a numinous Voice. Caring for someone else, even when we didn't feel like it, actually made us feel lighter, happier. We learned, in other words, that whether or not we believe it or feel like it, certain actions bring us closer to God.

Once you discover this truth, you're on your way back to spiritual practices.

And as we'll see in the final chapter, that may mean you're on your way back to some community of faith, the places where these ancient acts of devotion originated, and in which they are sustained generation after generation. Since houses of worship hold little appeal for an increasing number of people, you may not have bargained for any such return. But by now you've figured out that following Ariadne's thread often leads you to passages you couldn't have imagined.

TWENTY

Soul Friends

> One is not absolutely alone.… One cannot live and die
> for oneself alone. My life and my death are not purely
> and simply my own business. I live by and for others,
> and my death involves others.
>
> —Thomas Merton, *Conjectures of a Guilty Bystander*

hear the best stories at funerals.

Karl was a Stephen Minister in our congregation, St. Luke's. In a
year of training, Stephen Ministers learn how to care for people in
need—how to listen, how to offer help, how to be a compassionate
friend, often to those who have no one. Karl was just about the best.
Like all good pastors he had learned the lessons of love: you don't do
this work for thanks or recognition, and you are not responsible for
results. You do it because it is your gift, and you must offer it.

When Karl died we had a rousing funeral. Afterward at the re-
ception (where memorable stories often come out), a fellow Stephen
Minister told me how she had once called Karl to complain of a particularly needy person to whom she had been assigned. Was there no
way to trade this person for one less irritating?

Karl told her a story, and she passed it on to me as a tribute.

A priest went on retreat to a monastery and was really looking
forward to his time away. He got to the monastery and things

went pretty well, except that there was this guy named John who prayed next to him in the chapel and then was there in the refectory for meals. John was just sort of annoying, not the kind of person he wanted to be around that week. Nevertheless, he had a good retreat and went home.

Some months later he called the monastery to book another retreat. He said to the guest-house manager, "Yes, I'd like to book a retreat, but, if possible, can you book me for a week when that fellow John won't be there?"

And the guest house manager said, "Oh, Father, I'm so sorry. That won't be possible. John's here all the time. He's the one who teaches us how to love."

The final passage brings us into the chapel with John, into the refectory with John. True spirituality, which must first separate us from clan and community, always brings us back to a circle of belonging larger than our individual selves. In the same way that the apostle Paul encouraged his charges to "be imitators of me, as I am of Christ,"[1] we learn to imitate the compassion of Karl, even when we don't feel like it, when we want to trade the people we have been given to love for something better.

What Karl understood was the mystery of community. You don't choose the people in your circle; they are chosen by Someone else and given to you, just as you are chosen and given to them. As Henri Nouwen puts it, "Community is the place where the person you least want to live with always lives."[2]

Learning to love real people is only one of the lessons of communal life. It is here—in a particular community—that we learn the life of faith by doing it. Churches, synagogues, temples, mosques, and meeting houses are the places where spiritual practices originate and where they live.

If you wander into a Buddhist community, they'll ask you to sit for meditation, but you're just as likely to learn calligraphy or flower arranging or gardening as an intentional practice. A Sikh man gets up every day and puts on his turban. Wearing this is an act of solidarity with his community. Jews will show you how to observe Shabbat. They'll give you daily prayers, tell you what to eat and why. If you join a Christian community, they'll lead you into a pool of water, teach you to read Scripture, offer you bread and wine, and say, "The body and blood of our Lord Jesus Christ, given for you." Muslims will invite you to kneel in a line of worshipers—so close you're touching shoulders. You'll pray five times a day, and when Ramadan comes, you'll know it's time to fast till sundown. This is what communities do. They tell you what to do and when.

There's a wickedly wise line in George Herbert's poem "Lent": "The Scriptures bid us *fast;* the Church sayes, *now.*" The Bible clearly tells Christians to fast. No one denies it's a terrific idea, but since nobody wants to sit with the pangs of hunger while everybody else munches a cheeseburger, it becomes something we do in theory. We need the church to say, Do it *now.* Practice it. Ready or not. Like it or not. However, you don't sit with the pangs alone. You observe the fast in solidarity with your sisters and brothers.

Religious communities are home to all these life-giving customs, rituals, habits that take root in the heart. They are also, unfortunately, home to wooden beliefs, soulless practice, doctrinal boosterism, unimaginative sermons, and tired liturgy, not to mention people like John.

In a consumptive age of individual choice, many people are turning away from the old communities of faith. Still spiritually hungry, they raid ancient temples for the practices they like best and use them at their leisure. These time-tested acts of faith still work, but these practices were never meant for private use. They're designed as a package, held in trust by the faithful in this particular circle, and offered as a whole.

There are feast days and fast days. You can choose meditation because it soothes your anxiety, but you must also learn the works of mercy and how to care for someone else (and find to your amazement that you forget your anxiety). You can revel in prayers of radiant praise, but the gathered body will also lead you to prayers of confession and force you to face your own darkness. You won't choose fasting, works of mercy, and confession on your own; the community will *make* you. Against your will, hallelujah, you will be balanced, deepened, and protected from your own enormous powers of self-deception.

Many people in the throes of conventional faith shrink from the passage to community. That's because the itty-bitty *self* can only use spirituality for protection, solace, and affirmation. Its ego hasn't been unveiled. It is suspicious of anything that makes demands, forecloses choice, pulls you outside your comfort zone, introduces you as sister or brother to people you don't really know or like.

The power of community, though, is considerable. It can strangely enfold the cynical and skeptical, change people's hearts without their knowledge or consent. I see it all the time in the only community I really know, St. Luke's.

We are a regular Episcopal church. We have both mystics whose prayer lives are astonishing and believers who know only the rote petitions of our beloved Book of Common Prayer. There are people with doctorates in theology, and people who self-describe as churchgoing agnostics. We have parishioners who hug you at the Peace, and people who shudder at such a bohemian custom. There are some who worship faithfully each week, and many more (we call them C&Es) who come only at Christmas and Easter. We have an AA meeting with twenty-five people, and we have God only knows how many who more or less desperately need to be there but aren't. We have hundreds of people reading the entire Bible in one year, and others who complain that the church is getting too spiritual.

This isn't the Kingdom come. But I love it. It's one outpost of the Kingdom, and time after time I've seen it work its mystic powers.

On Wednesdays at 9:30 a.m. there's a healing service in our chapel. We offer the ancient rite of the laying on of hands and prayers for healing, either for yourself or for someone you love. I'm the rector of St. Luke's, but I know I am not the principal leader of this healing service. That distinction goes to a woman named Martha, a feisty, unchurchly woman who believes in the power of healing touch because she'd be dead without it. Martha has breast cancer, has for twenty years. She comes every Wednesday. In the summer she rides her blue Vespa. She comes for her own healing and brings with her all the wounded and lost lambs she finds along the way.

Three or four or five people kneel at the altar. "The tumor is back in my lung," the first man says. He can barely speak the dread words. His voice quavers. I anoint him, dip my thumb in healing oil, and smear the sign of the cross on his forehead. I lay my hands on his head, my thumbs at his temples. The group surrounds him now, laying hands on his shoulders, his back, his arms. We pray. We cry. In fact, there are so many tears that Martha asks if she can install Kleenex dispensers at either end of the altar rail. It sounds like a ghastly defacing of our oak-paneled chapel, but Martha pays a man to make matching oak boxes, mounts them on the walls, and drops a box of tissues in each. If tears are a sign of the Holy Spirit, we are covered.

After anointing and praying for each person at the rail, I often kneel with them. I hand the vial of oil to Martha and ask her to anoint me. I ask for the laying on of hands and the prayers. There is power here; we can all feel it. This is a charism, a grace that cannot exist on its own. It can thrive only in a family where there is no me without you. It only works if people put aside their habits and come just because someone else may need their gifts today, not because they plan to get anything out of it. It only works, that is, in community.

I thought I knew the power of that healing circle. I had no idea it was quietly transforming lives decades ago.

One of our members, Mark, has been around St. Luke's for forty or fifty years; he was married here. He's a cancer survivor who was, in Christopher Buckley's words, in "the Green Room to the river Styx"[3] and whose name, miraculously, was not called.

I watched Mark go off to divinity school. A few years later I was there at the St. Luke's altar when Mark was ordained a hospital chaplain. He already had a legendary ministry with cancer patients—many from the congregation, as well as friends, and friends of friends, who were drawn to this wounded healer.

I knew Mark only as a deep-souled man. I didn't know his whole story until just recently when he told me about his father.

"I was nineteen years old, in college," he said, "when my father was diagnosed with cancer. My mother could not deal with this frightening prospect, so it fell to me to walk with Dad through this. I talked to the doctors and translated all the medical data for my mother.

"We were nominal members of St. Luke's, but we never went to church except at the holidays. My father was a cradle Episcopalian, and my mother was solidly agnostic. I was baptized as a baby and confirmed in the Church of Canada when my father was posted there with the foreign service. I was in college in the sixties, mesmerized by intellectuals, filled with ideas my parents considered revolutionary. I had no interest in God, particularly.

"When I got married, I didn't want to give my children any religion. They should be able to choose for themselves, if they believed. That's how I left it.

"My dad lived with his illness for a lot of years, but as his cancer advanced, he often asked me to drive him to the healing service on Wednesdays. I'd rearrange my schedule so I could get him there.

"I remember sitting with him," Mark said, "not participating but keeping him company, watching his reactions week after week when he was well enough to go. Gradually the prayers became more familiar to me. I began to understand why he was pulled to this service—this small, intimate chapel, friends greeting him warmly each time. I sat in my pew and watched him go forward, kneel at the altar. It was clear that the laying on of hands meant everything to him. He was lifted up, even I could see that. He was comforted in a profound way.

"Slowly I came to realize that I was meeting God on Wednesdays in the chapel, though I was only here for Dad. Somehow the prayers became mine. I had become a believer."

The day finally came when Martha couldn't make it to the Wednesday service. Then we took the healing service to her home, anointed her there, and prayed for her ultimate healing, the final release that would unite her to her Creator, Redeemer, and Sanctifier.

The day of her funeral, her blue Vespa was leaning against the copper beech tree just off the cloister. I pulled a few tissues from the oaken dispensers and tucked them in the pocket of my robe. When I stood up to preach, I simply said, "Though I have no ecclesial authority to do so, nevertheless I rise to declare that Martha Kirk is a saint." The congregation laughed and thundered its applause.

If you can trust it, this is what a community will do—give you a set of time-tested practices that will change your life so gradually you won't know it's happening. Someone else will have to tell you that, like Moses come down from the mountain of God, your face is shining. You won't see it yourself. You don't need to believe in these acts; they work their blessing by another power—and in spite of your mental disposition one way or another.

One truth leads us inevitably to another. The soul progresses slowly, imperceptibly, by habitual practices that shape our hearts and transform our faces. But for this we need to give ourselves to a tradition bigger than ourselves, drawing us daily, weekly into worship, hospitality, prayer, healing, sacred reading, acts of mercy. In other words, this is a virtuous circle: following spiritual practices will lead you into a community somewhere, and the ordinary life of any faith community is its unique practice.

In her delicious memoir, *Take This Bread,* Sara Miles comes smack into communion with God just by stumbling into a church and doing what those people did. The book opens with these lines.

> One early, cloudy morning when I was forty-six, I walked into a church, ate a piece of bread, took a sip of wine. A routine Sunday activity for tens of millions of Americans—except that up until that moment I'd led a thoroughly secular life, at best indifferent to religion, more often appalled by its fundamentalist crusades. This was my first communion. It changed everything.
>
> Eating Jesus, as I did that day to my great astonishment, led me against all expectations to a faith I'd scorned and work I'd never imagined. The mysterious sacrament turned out to be not a symbolic wafer at all but actual food—indeed, the bread of life. In that shocking moment of communion, filled with a deep desire to reach for and become part of a body, I realized that what I'd been doing with my life all along was what I was meant to do: feed people.[4]

So she does. Sara Miles keeps receiving the bread of life and passing it to others. Then she opens a food pantry right at that altar and supplies hungry people with bread, with fruits and vegetables and cereal. One spiritual practice, receiving Holy Communion, led her inevitably to another, feeding the famished. All because she stumbled into a worshiping, working community.

So here I am at the close of this book, shooing you into some church or synagogue or storefront temple. There's a growing movement, hundreds of experimental communities, all flying under the banner of the Emerging Church—people meeting in homes, church basements, or even pubs. They may read Scripture, share their lives, and then go out to serve the homeless mentally ill. Many of these gatherings are reimagining the contemporary shape of spiritual community. In other words, you don't have to find your way into a Gothic edifice with ruffle-collared boy choirs, but I'm urging you to go somewhere bigger than you.

I know religious communities are out of favor. Many people who have moved on to more sophisticated and universal forms of spirituality are more or less above this. I know. But I believe this line from William Blake: "Eternity is in love with the productions of time." If we know anything of heaven, it is through the forms of earth.

The morning after he dreamed of a ladder propped on earth, leaning against the ramparts of heaven, Jacob took his stone pillow, set it up as an altar, poured oil over it, and called the place Bethel, "the house of God."

I too need an altar. Some ordinary stone, some plank of wood that has been sacred to a company of people long before I ever showed up on the planet.

I need oil, the kind we daub on children fresh from baptism, the kind we pour on the sick and suffering. Some people seem content with a higher power known only to the mind. I am happy for them. But I need sacred spaces that smell of old needlepoint cushions, heating oil, and candle wax. I want my higher power in real bread and wine. I want to confess my sins according to a fourth-century formula and have another human being pronounce God's pardon and absolution.

I want to eat pancakes on Shrove Tuesday, then lead a parade of children into the church garden and have them take turns with my spade, digging a miniature grave and burying the *Alleluia* for the forty days of Lent. It is hardly sublime, but it works—it satisfies my soul.

I'm not sure I actually believe in the Second Coming, so why do I secretly cry every Advent when I process into church singing, "Lo, he comes with clouds descending, once for our salvation slain"? It is so beautiful that I want it to be true. And it is, if not one day with clouds descending, then now with all of us singing and, on the last line, the chthonic rumble of the thirty-two-foot organ pipes shaking the foundations of Isaiah's latter-day, small-town temple.

The ultimate vision, it turns out, is a polar reverse. We don't glimpse the seventh heaven by booking a ride on the space shuttle, but by learning to see the infinite cloaked in ordinary. As Blake has it—

> To see a world in a grain of sand
> And a heaven in a wild flower,
> Hold infinity in the palm of your hand
> And eternity in an hour.
>
> A robin redbreast in a cage
> Puts all heaven in a rage.
> A dove house fill'd with doves and pigeons
> Shudders hell thro' all its regions.[5]

That is what the church on the corner offers you. A circle far too small for a group claiming to be a franchise of heaven, and a way of life that seems oddly preoccupied with the quotidian cycle of our days. Remember, "Eternity is in love with the productions of time."

Most people will take a pass on this last movement into a family of faith. They can't see past the bathos and boredom of it all. But you are ready for community, even a community in travail. You aren't looking for a perfect circle. You know how to forgive people for being small and broken and half-blind because you have forgiven all those things in yourself, which prepares you perfectly for a community of *blessedly human* human beings.

The Shrinking Door

> She came upon a low curtain she had not noticed
> before, and behind it was a little door about fifteen
> inches high: she tried the little golden key in the lock,
> and to her great delight it fitted!
>
> Alice opened the door and found that it led into
> a small passage, not much larger than a rat-hole: she
> knelt down and looked along the passage into the
> loveliest garden you ever saw.
>
> —Lewis Carroll, *Alice's Adventures in Wonderland*

I opened the prologue by telling you a secret. In closing, I will tell you one more.

Well, perhaps two.

The door to the Kingdom is narrow. And, you had better enter now.

The portals of heaven are very small. It would seem that everything about this infinite realm should be vast and spacious, and it is. Once you're inside. But for some reason all the passages to get in are quite tiny.

Jesus once said the aperture was roughly the size of a needle's eye. The gate, he said, is "narrow," and the road that leads to life is "narrow."[1] The same is true for the hatch.

I hesitate to tell you this, since I suspect by now you are starting to feel slightly cramped, but Jesus said, "Strive to enter through the narrow door; for many, I tell you, will try to enter and will not be able."[2]

Many people, especially those who think of themselves as progressive and broad minded, chafe at all this narrowness. How did the door to the Kingdom get so small? If God has posted over the door "Whosoever will may come," why isn't it as wide as humanity? It is especially galling for Jesus to say, explicitly, "For many, I tell you, will try to enter and will not be able." Why is God trying so hard to keep people out?

I have no idea how to answer any of those questions, but after staring for a long, long time at that beckoning door, I want to show you something I happened to notice.

First I have to tell you a story.

In my childhood home there was a door, almost a secret door. I remember the day I discovered it. I must have been seven or eight. It was at the bottom of the basement stairs. About five feet up the basement stone wall was a ledge, and beyond that a recessed area and a wooden panel wall—painted a dark green that had aged almost black.

I boosted myself up onto the ledge and discovered a latch hidden at the top of the panel. I flipped the latch, and the whole wall swung inward to reveal a tunnel. (It was actually the crawlspace around half the house, but I did not know that.) Armed with a flashlight, I crawled into its Stygian darkness, afraid of a horde of spiders I could see and a host of other creatures I was sure were lurking everywhere in this passage to Middle-earth. It was my secret passage, one I showed only to my younger brother John and my cousin Mark.

Twenty years ago I went back to my hometown of Yankton, South Dakota. I wanted to show my daughters where I grew up. I drove them to the three-story Victorian house where I had lived for the first fifteen years of my life. Over the years I had been back to the old homestead a few times but had never been inside. I knew the people who had originally bought the place, but they had since sold it to a couple no one in the family knew.

I intended only to show Maggy and Sharon the house and yard, but as we parked at the curb and got out, we noticed the owners washing their car by the garage. I wandered over and explained who I was—that I had lived in this house as a child and was bringing my kids back to see the old place.

They insisted we go inside.

I enjoyed showing the girls my bedroom and a few other features of a home that had always seemed my castle on a hill. But what I really wanted to see was the basement. No one offers to show you their unfinished basement, so I asked as politely as I could.

When I opened the basement door, the same musty smell rushed my nostrils. The stairs creaked beneath me, and near the bottom I had to duck my head. There I looked up hoping to see that panel, the wall that had swung open once so many years ago and invited me into its dim mysteries. But there was only a tiny door. Now I did not need to boost myself onto the ledge. From where I stood, I could easily flip the latch at the top. I pushed and the door yielded—to a cubbyhole. It was truly a *crawl* space! I was not sure whether I could squeeze through.

I stood there and wondered, *How did my secret door shrink? How did all this get so small?*

~

Something like this happens in the spirit world. Doors that used to seem wide and high arching begin to seem small. In fact, the door to the Kingdom, like everything in the eternal realm, is immutable, changeless, but over the course of your life it will appear to get smaller and smaller. Eventually you realize that it is not the door that has shrunk, but you who have grown larger and larger.

When you are very young, the entry to the Kingdom seems as vast as the sky. In your innocence you slip in and out without even knowing which world you are in. That's because you are almost naked, carrying nothing, racing free. But as you progress through life, you become more and more self-conscious. You learn to be ashamed of your nakedness, your nothingness, your carelessness.

Now everything small is passé. You want to be bigger. You want bigger clothes and shoes, a larger brain, a bigger voice. You need to carry a lot more things. You feel insecure without larger diplomas and deeds to bigger houses, keys to colossal cars. After a few terrible woundings you need a Kevlar vest to protect your heart. You're bulked up now.

You live like this for, who knows—thirty, forty, or fifty years, and over time you forget all about that beckoning door. When someone who doesn't know better mentions that door and the world that lies on its other side, you smile and politely change the subject.

Then it happens that you come once more upon that eternal door, either because of a great suffering that breaks your heart or a great love that could never be deserved or explained. But now the door seems small—too small. You stand there in all of your bigness and you realize: *In order to get through that door, I would have to drop all these things, strip down naked, and pray for a miracle the likes of which I have not seen since I traveled that narrow canal and came wailing into this world.*

—⚊—

The six passages that mark this odyssey are all narrow, some just a bit of a squeeze and some that strip your skin. But they are all tight—and this is what I want to tell you: they only get tighter. It is never, ever too late to make this journey because it is grace that prompts our will and makes us desire a passage into the Kingdom, and it is grace alone that pulls us through. But it gets harder and harder the longer you wait, the more you hang on to all you carry.

I hope you are still holding Ariadne's slender, guiding thread, the one I handed you at the outset. It is all you need. Your arrival has already been assured.

But go—go now.

GRATITUDES

efore I could write this book, I had to live it. Which means I had to make a lot of mistakes, write not one, but two versions that would not breathe on their own. It gives me special joy, then, to thank the many people who kept breathing new life into this book.

Pam Anderson, my wife and seven-time author, was the first to read earlier manuscripts and suggest that I write this book and tell this story in a different voice—my own. Since I thought I already had it right, I was resistant. I want to thank Pam for listening to all my arguments and justifications, and insisting that a better book was still inside me.

Sarah Jane Freymann, my agent, offered timely advice and gave the book its title. And when I needed help finding a new direction, Sarah Jane directed me to my former editor, Joanne Wyckoff, who spent weeks poring over my manuscript, telling me how to turn what was essentially a textbook into an illustrated guidebook. Without Pam, Sarah Jane, and Joanne, this book would not be breathing on its own. Thank you.

Dave Kopp, my editor, believed not only in the manuscript but in me. I am deeply indebted to his wise direction and the deft editing of Elisa Stanford, for any coherence and unity this book possesses.

I am grateful to Pamela Shoup, the production editor, and Rose Decaen, the copy editor, for catching all the things I missed, and making many opaque sentences clear; and to Amy Partain, for researching and editing the endnotes. My thanks to all the great people at Convergent Books who have worked on behalf of this project: Kendall Davis, Ashley Boyer, and Allison O'Hara.

Writing is a solitary practice and encouragement is a balm. My two daughters, Margaret Keet and Sharon Damelio—always the apples of my eye—have loved and cheered me without measure. And my two brothers, Michael and John, read earlier versions of this book and offered valuable insights.

Many friends have supported my work as a writer, encouraging me, and throwing impromptu celebrations at key points along the "deadline" process. I want to thank especially Art and Terrie Brown, Bob Dixon, Cliff Nesbit, Jerry Rardin, Robert Schroeder, and Alec and Gail Wiggin.

As a writing pastor, I live and offer my ministry among the people of Saint Luke's Parish, Darien, Connecticut. The really good sheep show the shepherd how to care for the flock, and Saint Luke's is filled with really great sheep. They've taught me how to love and care for the people of God—and they've cared for me and my family. I will always be grateful. I want especially to thank my executive assistant, Judy Barnett, without whose help, insight, and advice I would not have been able to be both a pastor and a writer.

Finally, I thank my parents. My mother, Aldoris Anderson, "went home to be with the Lord"—as we used to say in the Baptist church— fourteen years ago. I am a Christian because of her faith, and my love of music and words is her legacy in me. My father, Gerald Anderson, turned ninety-four this year. He is what I have always hoped to be: a man of integrity, generosity, compassion, and humility. As his family grows to scores of grandchildren and great-grandchildren, all with diverse social, political, and religious viewpoints, my father continues to model for us how to hold steadfastly to his own beliefs, yet hold open a cherished place at the family table for every one of us. He will not agree with some of what I write in this book, but when I see him next he will still love me and kiss me and own me as his beloved son, then sit me down and beat me at gin rummy.

Prologue

1. Ernest Hemingway, *A Farewell to Arms* (1929; repr., New York: Scribner, 2012), 318.

Chapter 1

1. Matthew 16:25.
2. James Hillman, *The Force of Character: And the Lasting Life* (New York: Ballantine, 1999), 129.
3. See James Fowler, *Stages of Faith: The Psychology of Human Development and the Quest for Meaning* (New York: Harper Collins, 1981).

Chapter 2

1. Isaiah 40:6, NKJV.
2. Ecclesiastes 1:2, KJV.
3. Paul Tillich, *Dynamics of Faith* (New York: Harper & Row, 1957), 1.
4. Peter De Vries, *The Blood of the Lamb* (Chicago: University of Chicago Press, 2005), vii.
5. Dante Alighieri, "Inferno," *The Divine Comedy* (New York: Oxford University Press, 1961), 23.
6. Reynolds Price, *A Whole New Life* (New York: Simon & Schuster, 1994), 184.
7. Maezumi Roshi, quoted in Robert A. Johnson, *Transformation: Understanding the Three Levels of Masculine Consciousness* (New York: Harper Collins, 1991), 84.

Chapter 3

1. Mark 10:17.
2. See Mark 10:19–21.

3. Nikos Kazantzakis, *Report to Greco* (New York: Simon & Schuster, 1965), 222.
4. William Willimon, *On a Wild and Windy Mountain* (Nashville: Abingdon Press, 1984), 90.

Chapter 4

1. Richard Rohr, *Falling Upward: A Spirituality for the Two Halves of Life* (San Francisco: Jossey-Bass, 2011), 21.
2. John Bunyan, *The Pilgrim's Progress,* Oxford World Classics (New York: Oxford University Press, 2009), 13.
3. Colman McCarthy, *Inner Companions* (Camarillo, CA: Acropolis Books, Inc., 1975), 173.
4. William S. Burroughs, *Word Virus: The William S. Burroughs Reader,* eds. James Grauerholz and Ira Silverberg (New York: Grove Press, 1998), xix.

Chapter 5

1. Sinclair Lewis, *Babbitt* (New York: Signet Classic from New American Library, 1961), 319.
2. May Sarton, "Now I Become Myself," *Collected Poems 1930–1993* (New York: W. W. Norton, 1974), 156.
3. Donald Spoto, *Reluctant Saint: The Life of Francis of Assisi* (New York: Penguin, 2002), 54.
4. Mark 1:12.
5. Murray Bowen, *Family Therapy in Clinical Practice* (Lanham, MD: Rowman & Littlefield, 1992), 461.

Chapter 6

1. Clarissa Pinkola Estés, *Women Who Run with the Wolves* (New York: Signet Classic from New American Library, 1961), 319.
2. Murray Bowen, *Family Therapy in Clinical Practice* (Lanham, MD: Rowman & Littlefield, 1985), 108.
3. Karen Armstrong, *Islam: A Short History* (New York: Modern Library, 2002), 13.

4. Armstrong, *Islam,* 13–14.
5. Armstrong, *Islam,* 14.
6. Luke 14:26.
7. Mark 3:20–21, 32–35, NIV.

Chapter 7
1. Proverbs 27:6, NIV.
2. *Virginia Seminary Journal,* published by The Protestant Episcopal Theological Seminary in Virginia, Alexandria. February 2007, 30.
3. Cathy Ladman, quoted in Richard Dawkins, *The God Delusion* (New York: Mariner Books, 2008), 195.
4. Matthew 7:3.
5. Genesis 1:26; 2:9.

Chapter 8
1. Jennifer Scanlon, *Bad Girls Go Everywhere: The Life of Helen Gurley Brown* (New York: Penguin), 143.
2. Christopher Buckley, *Losing Mum and Pup* (Toronto: McClelland & Steward, 2009), 39.
3. Albert L. Winseman, "Eternal Destinations: Americans Believe in Heaven, Hell," Gallup.com, May 25, 2004.
4. John Newton, "Amazing Grace," *Olney Hymns,* 1779, public domain.
5. Michael Guillen, *Five Equations That Changed the World: The Power and Poetry of Mathematics* (New York: Hyperion, 1995), 248–50.
6. C. S. Lewis, *A Grief Observed* (New York: Bantam Books, 1983), 28–29.
7. Albert Einstein, quoted in Thomas M. Dicken and Rem B. Edward, *Dialogues on Values and Centers of Value: Old Friends, New Thoughts* (The Netherlands: Rodopi, 2001), 34.
8. John 6:40, NIV.
9. Luke 9:58–62, MSG.
10. Matthew 13:44.

11. Matthew 13:45–46.
12. Annie Dillard, *Teaching a Stone to Talk: Expeditions and Encounters* (New York: HarperCollins, 1982), 52.
13. Albert Camus, *The Fall* (New York: Alfred A Knopf, First Vintage International Edition, 1991), 111.
14. Slavoj Žižek, *Hegel and the Shadow of Dialectical Materialism* (London: Verso, 2012), 209.
15. Chester P. Michael, *An Introduction to Spiritual Direction* (Mahwah, NJ: Paulist Press, 2004), 63.

Chapter 9

1. Hans Staffner, *What Does It Mean to Be a Christian?* (Mumbai: Society of St. Paul, 1978), 24.
2. T. S. Eliot, *T. S. Eliot: Collected Poems* (New York: Harcourt Brace: 1991), 79.
3. Patrick Kavanagh, "Pegasus," *Irish Literature: A Reader,* ed. Maureen O'Rourke Murphy & James MacKillop (Syracuse, NY: Syracuse University Press, 1987), 310.
4. *The Freud-Jung Letters,* ed. William McGuire, abridged edition (Princeton, NJ: Princeton University Press, 1994), xxx.
5. Parker J. Palmer, *A Hidden Wholeness* (San Francisco: Jossey-Bass, 2004), 58–59.
6. Javier Melloni, SJ, *The Exercises of St. Ignatius Loyola in the Western Tradition* (Bodmin, England: MPG Books, Ltd., 2000), 29.

Chapter 10

1. Bryce Courtenay, *The Power of One* (New York: Ballantine Books, 2008), 8–45.
2. Courtenay, *The Power of One,* 46–47.
3. Robert A. Fles, "The Weird, the Strange, and the Quirky (Kid)," *Independent School Magazine,* Fall 2009. www.nais.org/Magazines-Newsletters/ISMagazine/Pages/The-Weird-the-Strange-and-the-Quirky-Kid.aspx.

4. Thomas Merton, *New Seeds of Contemplation* (New York: New Directions, 1961), xi.

5. Thomas Keating, *Foundations for Centering Prayer and the Christian Contemplative Life* (London: Continuum, 2006), 166–67.

6. Romans 7:24.

7. Luke 9:23–24, NIV.

8. Anthony DeMello *Wake Up to Life* (7-CD set recorded live at Fordham University, 1986), Disc one.

9. Winston Churchill, *Never Give In! The Best of Winston Churchill's Speeches* (New York: Hyperion, 2003), 139–40.

10. James Hollis, *Finding Meaning in the Second Half of Life: How to Finally, Really Grow Up* (New York: Gotham Books, 2005), 70.

11. Hollis, *Finding Meaning,* 71.

12. Augustine, quoted in Leo J. Elders S.V.D., *The Philosophical Theology of Thomas Aquinas* (Leiden, The Netherlands: E. J. Brill, 1990), 171.

13. St. Patrick's Breastplate, quoted in John Pritchard, *Leading Intercessions: Creative Ideas for Public and Private Prayer* (Collegeville, MN: Liturgical Press, 1994), 142.

Chapter 11

1. John de Yepes, *St. John of the Cross* (London: Cambridge University Press, 1932), 33.

2. Dr. Dan Gottlieb, "Voices of the Family." This is a paraphrase of the radio interview based on the author's recollection.

3. "A Grandfather's Message to His Autistic Son," NPR Books, June 25, 2010. www.npr.org/templates/story/story.php?storyId=128 086851.

4. *The Little Flowers of St. Francis of Assisi,* trans. Sir Thomas Walker Arnold (London: Chatto & Windus, 1908), 60–64.

5. *Milk,* directed by Gus Van Sant (2008; Universal City, CA: Focus Features, 2009).

6. Tsultrim Allione, *Feeding Your Demons: Ancient Wisdom for Resolving Inner Conflict* (New York: Little, Brown and Company, 2008).
7. Mark 12:34.
8. Robert Bly, quoted in Richard Rohr, *On the Threshold of Transformation: Daily Meditations for Men* (Chicago: Loyola Press), 211.
9. Martin Cooper-White, *The Comeback God* (Minneapolis: Augsburg Press, 2009), 123.

Chapter 12
1. Katherine Paterson, *Bridge to Terabithia* (New York: Crowell, 1977).
2. William James, *The Varieties of Religious Experience: A Study in Human Nature* (Rockville, MD: Arc Manor, 2008), 46.
3. Ezekiel 37:1–14.
4. *Buddhism: The Illustrated Guide,* ed. Kevin Trainor, (New York: Oxford University Press, 2004), 29.
5. John 3:3, NIV.
6. Romans 13:11.
7. Martin Luther King, Jr., "But, If Not," (sermon, Ebenezer Baptist Church, November 5, 1967), quoted in Bob Buford, *Beyond Halftime: Practical Wisdom for Your Second Half* (Grand Rapids, MI: Zondervan, 2008), 23.
8. *Fyodor Dostoevsky,* ed. Harold Bloom, (New York: Haights Cross Communications, 2003), 6–9.

Chapter 13
1. Gene Weingarten, *The Fiddler in the Subway: The Story of the World-Class Violinist Who Played for Handouts* (New York: Simon & Schuster, 2010).
2. T. S. Eliot, *The Waste Land* (Boston: Houghton Mifflin Harcourt, 1971), 136.
3. Dante Alighieri, *The Divine Comedy,* "Inferno" (New York: Oxford University Press, 1961), 49.
4. Exodus 3:3.

5. William Butler Yeats, *Yeats's Poetry, Drama, and Prose*, ed. James Pethica (New York: W. W. Norton & Company, 2000), 361.

6. Joseph T. Kelley, *Saint Augustine of Hippo: Selections from Confessions and Other Essential Writings* (Woodstock, VT: Skylight Paths Publishing, 2010), 79.

7. Joe Paprocki, *Seven Keys to Spiritual Wellness: Enriching Your Faith by Strengthening the Health of Your Soul* (Chicago: Loyola Press, 2012), 24.

8. Picasso, quoted in Duane Elgin, *Voluntary Simplicity: Toward a Way of Life That Is Outwardly Simple, Inwardly Rich* (New York: HarperCollins, 2010), 20.

9. Meister Eckhart, quoted in Rabbi Edwin Goldberg, *Saying No and Letting Go: Jewish Wisdom on Making Room for What Matters Most* (Woodstock, VT: Jewish Lights, 2013), 38.

10. Antoine de Saint-Exupéry, *Airman's Odyssey* (Boston: Houghton Mifflin Harcourt, 2012), 39.

11. Emily Dickinson, *Poetry for Young People: Emily Dickinson*, ed. Frances S. Bolin (New York: Sterling, 1994), 7.

Chapter 14

1. John Cheever, quoted in Walker Percy, *Lost in the Cosmos: The Last Self-Help Book* (New York: Picador, 1983), 179.

2. Russell, "What Is an Agnostic?" *Look* (1953), quoted in "Bertrand Russell Society Archives," Bertrand Russell Society, http://bertrandrussell.org/archives/BRSpapers/2012/agnostic.php.

3. Walenc James, *Immunization: The Reality Behind the Myth*, vol. 3 (Greenwood, 1995), 134.

4. Fyodor Dostoevsky, *The Brothers Karamazov* (New York: Macmillan, 1922), 247.

5. Peter De Vries, *The Blood of the Lamb* (Chicago: University of Chicago Press, 2005), 243.

6. Woody Allen, quoted in Edward Kessler, *What Do Jews Believe?: The Customs and Culture of Modern Judaism* (New York: Walker, 2007), 66.

7. Horatio Spafford, "It Is Well with My Soul," 1873, public domain.

8. Numbers 21:9.

9. Marcel Proust, quoted in Larry Chang, comp. and ed., *Wisdom for the Soul: Five Millennia of Prescriptions for Spiritual Healing* (Washington, DC: Gnosophia, 2006), 687.

10. Thomas Merton, *The Seven Storey Mountain* (Orlando: Harcourt, 1948), 91.

11. Hans Ur von Balthasar, quoted in "Richard's Daily Meditation," Center for Action and Contemplation, http://archive.constant contact.com/fs028/1103098668616/archive/1106776211327.html.

12. Roger Rosenblatt, "Faithfully Yours," *Modern Maturity* (May–June 1995), 36.

13. Alan Watts, *On Helping Others,* quoted in Billionquotes.com, www .billionquotes.com/index.php/Alan_Watts.

14. Julian of Norwich, *Revelations of Divine Love* (Cambridge, MA: Harvard College Library, 2005), 57.

Chapter 15

1. Matthew 16:2–3, MSG.

2. Luke 1:35.

3. Thomas Keating, *Invitation to Love* (New York: Continuum International, 2006), 44–46.

4. See Genesis 32.

5. James W. Fowler, *The Stages of Faith* (New York: HarperCollins, 1981), 198.

6. Rainer Maria Rilke, "A Man Watching," *News of the Universe,* comp. Robert Bly (San Francisco: Sierra Club, 1995), 121–22.

Chapter 16

1. Dylan Thomas, quoted in Matthew Parris, "Bore for England? Sometimes You Just Have To," *The Times,* December, 24, 2009, www.thetimes.co.uk/tto/opinion/columnists/matthewparris /article2044517.ece.

2. Westminster Catechism, question 98, www.cambridgepres.org.uk /cat/cat98.html.

3. Baltimore Catechism, question 1099, www.baltimore-catechism .com/lesson28.htm.

4. Brian Cavanaugh, *The Sower's Seeds: 120 Inspiring Stories for Preaching, Teaching, and Public Speaking* (Mahwah, NJ: Paulist Press, 2004), 40.

5. Dag Hammarskjöld, quoted in Manuel Fröehlich, *Political Ethics and the United Nations: Dag Hammarskjöld as Secretary-General* (New York: Routledge, 2008), 85.

6. Jean Pierre de Caussade, *The Sacrament of the Present Moment* (New York: HarperCollins, 1989).

7. Paul Tillich, quoted in Stanley Grenz, *Theology for the Community of God* (Grand Rapids, MI: William B. Eerdmans, 2000), 79.

8. Cynthia Bourgeault, *Centering Prayer and Inner Awakening* (Lanham, MD: Cowley, 2004), 23–24.

9. For the idea of the "letting-go muscle," I am indebted to Cynthia Bourgeault, who speaks of a "'muscle' of surrender" in *Centering Prayer and Inner Awakening,* 24, 162. For more information on Centering Prayer, go to contemplativeoutreach.com.

10. Brother Lawrence, "The Practice of the Presence of God" in *Devotional Classics,* ed. Richard J. Foster and James Bryan Smith, (New York: Harper San Francisco, 1993), 83.

11. Peggy Rosenthal, *Knit One, Purl a Prayer: A Spirituality of Knitting* (Brewster, MA: Paraclete Press, 2011), 8.

12. Romans 8:28.

13. Pierre Teilhard de Chardin, *The Divine Milieu* (Portland, OR: Sussex Academic Press, 2004), 50–51.

Chapter 17

1. Matthew 18:21, NIV.

2. Matthew 18:22, NKJV.

3. Matthew 18:23–35.

4. *Daily Readings with the Desert Fathers* (Springfield, IL: Templegate, 1990), 27.

5. Martin Luther, quoted in Martin Manser, ed., *The Westminster Collection of Christian Quotations* (Louisville, KY: Westminster John Knox Press, 2001), 114.

6. See Matthew 5:11; see Luke 6:29; Matthew 5:44.

Chapter 18

1. Richard Rohr, *Everything Belongs: The Gift of Contemplative Prayer* (New York: Crossroad, 2003).

2. Carl Jung, quoted in David Richo, *Daring to Trust: Opening Ourselves to Real Love & Intimacy* (Boston: Shambhala, 2010), 180.

3. Casalnnie O. Henry, *Avoiding the Fear Trap* (Mustang, OK: Tate Publishing, LLC, 2010), 128.

4. Thomas Keating, *Foundations for Centering Prayer and the Christian Contemplative Life* (New York: Continuum International, 2006), 111.

5. Harold Kushner, *Overcoming Life's Disappointments* (New York: Random House, 2006), 97.

6. Exodus 31:18.

7. Exodus 32:19.

8. Exodus 34:1.

9. Exodus 34:27–28.

Chapter 19

1. Leon Wieseltier, *Kaddish* (New York: Knopf, 1998), vii.

2. Wieseltier, *Kaddish,* vii.

3. Aristotle, quoted in "The Nichomachean Ethics" in *Ethics: Selections from Classical and Contemporary Writers* (Boston: Wadsworth, Cengage Learning, 2012), 77.

4. C. S. Lewis, *The Complete C. S. Lewis Signature* (New York: HarperCollins, 2002), 152.

5. Martin Smith, *Compass and Stars,* (New York: Seabury, 2007), 4.

6. Ezekiel 33:31.

7. Matthew 7:24–27.

8. Acts 9:2.

9. James 2:20, NKJV.

10. Erich Fromm, *The Art of Loving* (New York: Harper & Row, 1962), 108.

11. Atul Gawande, "The Learning Curve," *The New Yorker,* January 28, 2002, 56.

12. "The Learning Curve," 56.

13. Albert Ellis obituary, *The New York Times,* July 25, 2007.

14. *The Paris Review,* Issues 101–103, 1986, 60.

15. Michael Wilson, "After Miracle on Hudson, Many Promises to Keep," *The New York Times,* January 14, 2010, www.nytimes.com /2010/01/15/nyregion/15promises.html?pagewanted=all&_r=0.

16. Eugene Peterson, *A Long Obedience in the Same Direction: Discipleship in an Instant Society,* 2nd ed. (Downers Grove, IL: InterVarsity Press, 2000).

Chapter 20

1. 1 Corinthians 11:1.

2. Henri Nouwen, with Michael J. Christensen and Rebecca J. Laird, *Spiritual Direction: Wisdom for the Long Walk of Faith* (New York: Harper One, 2006), 113.

3. Christopher Buckley, *Losing Mum and Pup* (Toronto: McClelland & Steward, 2009), 5.

4. Sara Miles, *Take This Bread* (New York: Ballantine, 2007), xi.

5. William Blake, "Auguries of Innocence," *The Complete Poetry & Prose of William Blake,* ed. David V. Erdman, (New York: Anchor, revised edition, 1997), 490.

Epilogue

1. Matthew 7:13.

2. Luke 13:24.